MW00638086

The MONOCLE
Travel Guide Series

Amsterdam

For more information, please visit *gestalten.com*

Bibliographic information published by the Deutsche Nationalbibliothek: The Deutsche Nationalbibliothek lists this publication in the Deutsche Nationalbibliografie; detailed bibliographic data are available online at *dnb.d-nb.de*

This book was printed on paper certified by the FSC®

Monocle editor in chief and chairman: *Tyler Brûlé*
Monocle editor: *Andrew Tuck*
Books editor: *Joe Pickard*
Guide editor: *Mikaela Aitken*

Designed by *Monocle*
Proofreading by *Monocle*
Typeset in *Plantin & Helvetica*

Printed by *Offsetdruckerei Grammlich, Pliezhausen*

Made in Germany

Updated edition published by *gestalten*, Berlin 2020
ISBN 978-3-89955-873-9

© Die Gestalten Verlag GmbH & Co. KG, Berlin 2020

Welcome
—— Alluring Amsterdam

Boats bobbing on canals, rows of colourful houses, cosy pubs and friendly locals: it's easy to be swayed by the patent charms of the *Dutch capital*. But dwell a little longer and you'll see that the city's appeal runs much deeper.

The compact centre is a medley of heritage-listed buildings, independent retail and a growing collection of *top tables*. Just a 10-minute cycle further out (most places are a 10-minute cycle away here) will land you in vibrant, evolving neighbourhoods that meld bold contemporary architecture with socially conscious *Amsterdam School* housing developments. Sprawling green spaces pop with colour when the *tulips bloom* in spring. And across the city there's a compelling cultural offering, including a hefty hoard of works by the *Dutch masters*, art deco cinemas and post-industrial lots repurposed for *gigs and exhibitions.*

But like all cities, Amsterdam has its shortfalls. It has a reputation for badly behaved visitors and a touristy centre dominated by tacky shops and insalubrious types. However, the local government is working hard to mend this and position the city as a *haven for business* by making the most of its highly educated English-speaking population and low corporate taxes.

Amsterdam continues to build on its reputation as a *dynamic and welcoming* place. So turn the page and join us on a journey through the cobbled streets and smooth snaking bikeways of this wonderful city. — (M)

Contents
—— Navigating the city

Use the key below to help navigate the guide section by section.

- **H** Hotels
- **F** Food and drink
- **R** Retail
- **T** Things we'd buy
- **E** Essays
- **C** Culture
- **D** Design and architecture
- **S** Sport and fitness
- **W** Walks

Map
—— Lay of the land and sea

The Netherlands shouldn't exist: more than a quarter of the country lies beneath sea level, including its capital (the parliament may sit in The Hague but this is the capital city). Yet by the 13th century, fishermen based themselves on the peat swamps near the Amstel river and built a dam, giving rise to Amsterdam.

In the Middle Ages the series of dykes and dams expanded, creating pieces of low-lying land reclaimed from the sea and allowing Amsterdam to expand into a small port town. Trade boomed in the 16th and 17th centuries and the subsequent wealth saw the network of canals and houses more than double.

The industrial revolution saw the addition of a west entrance to the harbour and another belt of land, including the three islands that house Centraal station. Today town-planners are looking to the harbour to develop dynamic neighbourhoods in the Noord and Eastern Docklands, while Zuidas in the south is bolstering its role as the central business district.

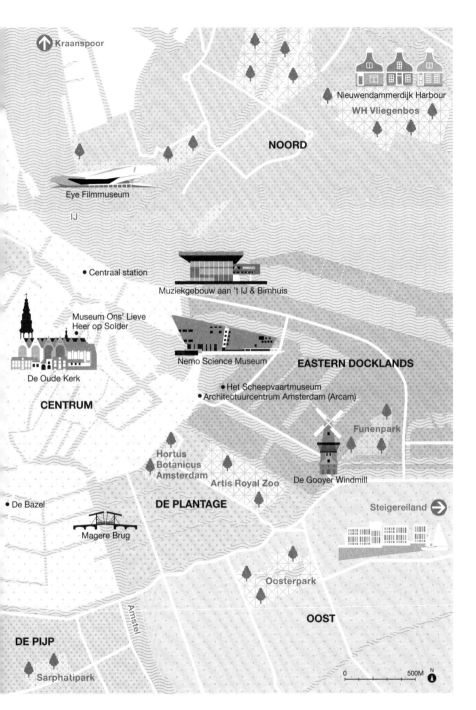

Need to know
—— Defining the Dutch

Amsterdam is considered to be one of the most liberal cities in the world but there are a few nuances to wrap your head around before arriving. From kissing three times to ordering the right-sized beer, here are a few handy tips and fast facts to help you blend in with the locals.

Greetings
Meet and greet

When in a business setting or meeting someone for the first time, a firm handshake will suffice. If you're meeting a friend, a trio of kisses is the go-to greeting. In general the Dutch don't beat around the bush but don't mistake this directness for poor manners. Quite the contrary: a polite demeanour is very much appreciated. Finally, when it comes to attending a birthday party, be sure to congratulate all of the family members on the anniversary as well – and they will likely congratulate you right back.

Urban planning
Building a case

There's little room for new development in the Unesco World Heritage-listed 17th-century canal ring that circles the city centre. As such, town-planners are working to solve the housing shortage by attracting residential developments to post-industrial areas through urban-renewal projects and commissioning attractive contemporary public buildings. To see this change in action venture out from the centre and visit the Eye Filmmuseum in Noord, the Westergasfabriek in Westerpark and Bimhuis in the Eastern Docklands. Also keep an eye on the central business district of Zuidas, which has become a favoured base for international headquarters.

Hold on folks, we're turning right!

Cycling
Pedal to the metal

With the city centre's one-way street system, driving can be a frustrating experience – so cycling is by far the best way to get around. Remember to indicate your direction by sticking out a hand and bear in mind that traffic from the right has right of way. Helmets aren't compulsory but lights at night are. Also be sure to pedal hard: if an Amsterdammer spots you dallying in the bike lane you'll likely cop an earful.

Liberal values
The new normal

We all think of Amsterdam as a liberal city but its liberal policies may have more to do with pragmatism than tolerance. To the Dutch, choosing to turn a blind eye to cannabis and decriminalising prostitution is sensible: it removes the lure of vice and repositions it as mundane. However, the city is still trying to find such a balance with the rowdy stag and hen dos. And take note: a coffeeshop is not for caffeine.

Money
Cash in hand

Maestro is king in the city and the card machines used by retailers and smaller cafés don't always accept Visa or Amex. To avoid an awkward conversation about what will be left as collateral while you dash to the nearest ATM, be sure to carry a little extra cash. Tipping isn't customary but if you do happen to experience excellent service – it's surprisingly sporadic in the capital – then 10 per cent is recommended.

Beer
Raise a glass

Amsterdam is the birthplace of some of the world's most famous beer brands. Ask for *een biertje* (a beer) in a pub and you'll be given the house lager on tap, often Amstel or Heineken. The typical Dutch beer glass is a half pint – ordering a full pint is a faux pas – and should be topped with about 2cm of foam. This foam is part of the beer experience; locals call foamless beer "dead beer". Ask for an *amsterdammertje* if you want your beer served in a traditional Dutch glass.

The best solution to any problem – a healing draft of lager

Now that boat looks like a nice place to perch

Language
Dutch masters

Most Dutch speak at least two languages and they're among the best non-native English speakers in the world. Children start learning English from the age of 10 and then take on at least one other foreign language in high school (often German, French or Spanish). This, alongside the low barriers to entry, is what attracts so much foreign investment to the city. Plus, all English TV shows and films are subtitled rather than dubbed, making a trip to the cinema a breeze.

Why 'IJ' is not a typo
Learning the lingo

When it comes to English speakers learning the Dutch language, you'll notice that many words – such as colours, vegetables and fruits – have Germanic roots. Reading proves slightly easier than interpreting the guttural speech. One important nuance to note is the use of "IJ" as a single letter. It's pronounced along the lines of "aey" and is derived from a word that means water. It's also the official name given to the harbour and river.

Terrace culture
Alfresco drinking

As soon as there's the slightest hint of spring in the air Amsterdammers spill out onto the terraces of cafés and restaurants. The Dutch even have a special saying for this affinity with perching outdoors: *een terrasje pakken*. This translates as "take a terrace" but it's commonly used as a verb to suggest to friends or colleagues that you grab a drink outside. Fitting for a city with picturesque canals and parks aplenty.

Food and drink
Wine and dine

The Dutch have peculiar food preferences. They like their bread with all sorts of spreads and sprinkles and enjoy starchy meals such as *hutspot* (potatoes, carrots and onions) and *andijviestamppot* (potatoes and endive), as well as fried snacks that are sometimes dispensed from vending machines (*see page 32*). If you're craving a meal at one of the city's top tables be sure to call ahead because most are rammed night after night. Peak time is between 18.30 and 19.30 and kitchens close relatively early.

Why editors have a problem with waffle is beyond me

Hotels
—— Where
to stay

The hotel selection
in Amsterdam is as
much a journey into the
architectural ethos of
the city as it is an offering
of accommodation.
You'll find modern and
towering chains if that's
what you're hankering
after (Hotel Okura fits the
bill) but don't overlook
Amsterdam's more unique
options. In keeping
with the most intriguing
buildings around the
city, these hotels take
advantage of existing
structures in pragmatic
but respectful fashion.
There are hotels that
consist of more than
20 buildings tethered
together, that occupy the
repurposed sites of music
schools, juvenile detention
centres and newspaper
offices, or that simply
enjoy architecture dating
back to the 17th century.
    Also worth a look is
the new wave of design
hotels that skew towards
a younger clientele, with
more affordable rooms and
creative concepts. Check
in and check them out.

①
Hotel V Fizeaustraat,
Watergraafsmeer
The 1970s with a twist

The Fizeaustraat branch, which
opened in 2017, is Hotel V's third
location in the capital. It's a little
further afield, in the east's developing
district of Watergraafsmeer, but
it's only a 10-minute taxi ride from
the canal ring and in our opinion
the standout of the trio.
    In-house designer Mirjam
Espinosa has seamlessly blended
a modish 1970s aesthetic into the
boxy Piet Zanstra building and
carefully chosen furnishings that
echo the surrounding greenery.
All 91 rooms are finished with
hexagonal solid-oak parquet floors,
pebble-grey linens and woollen
tapestries. The ever-friendly staff
are on hand 24/7 to assist with any
requests, including bike rental,
international newspapers, laundry
and in-room massages.
2 Fizeaustraat, 1097 SC
+31 (0)20 662 3233
hotelvfizeaustraat.nl

MONOCLE COMMENT: The hotel may
feel like it's out in the sticks but
that doesn't deter Amsterdammers
from dining in Jeroen van Spall's
always-teeming restaurant, The
Lobby. The house special is
flammkuche ("flame cake")
from the Alsace region.

2

Pulitzer Hotel, Centrum
Room for variety

Peter Pulitzer's hotel first opened in 1970 in the retail district of De 9 Straatjes and, after extensive renovations, reopened in 2016. The canal-side space spans 25 connected 17th and 18th-century townhouses with 225 rooms, 19 of them suites.

No two rooms are the same: architect and creative director Jacu Strauss stayed in each and every one to mull over the fit-out. "We chose a range of styles and finishes that suit the buildings' 400 years of history," he says. The result is an eclectic mix, with velvet-upholstered armchairs sitting alongside modern desks. One thing is consistent: each room has its own marble bathroom.
315-331 Prinsengracht, 1016 GZ
+31 (0)20 523 5235
pulitzeramsterdam.com

MONOCLE COMMENT: It's hard to beat the extra space and canal-side views in the suites. A handful offer guests a private entrance and can be booked upon request.

I suppose there are worse places to get lost

③
Morgan & Mees, Westerpark
Lesson in luxury

This petite hotel may sit on the
corner of two congested streets but
its nine rooms are relaxed, good-
looking and, most importantly,
welcoming. The former 17th-
century school was transformed
by hospitality entrepreneurs
Myrthe Slotemaker and Roger
Peetoom, along with designer
Marius Haverkamp in 2014.
Peetoom's wife, Anne Claus, led the
interior design, choosing parqueted
wooden floors, mid-century chairs
and modern artwork to decorate
the rooms.
    When booking it's worth opting
for the single-storey rooms as the
sleeping arrangements in the
duplexes are slightly more
cramped. The bar and restaurant
on the ground floor offer room
service or, if the weather's good,
head to the terrace at the front.
2-6 Tweede Hugo de Grootstraat,
1052 LC
+ 31 (0)20 233 4930
morganandmees.com

MONOCLE COMMENT: The boutique
nature of the hotel lends itself well
to slightly longer stints in the city.
The downside is that there's no
gym or spa but it's in a prime spot
for a jog around the canal ring
instead (*see page 127*).

④
The Hoxton, Centrum
Mid-century marvel

The Hoxton is another newcomer
to the host of design hotels in De 9
Straatjes, having opened its doors
in 2015. Inconspicuous from the
street, the 111 rooms sit within five
interjoining canal houses, one of
which was the residence of the
city's mayor in the 17th century
(two more classically designed
concept rooms are in this section
of the building and can be booked
upon request).
    Each room is different but the
reupholstered vintage furniture
and exposed copper pipes in the
bathrooms neatly tie the hotel's
cosy mid-century theme together.
If you're after a quick start to the
day, hang your breakfast bag
outside your door in the evening
to have complimentary yoghurt,
granola, banana and fresh orange
juice waiting for you in the morning.
255 Herengracht, 1016 BJ
+ 31 (0)20 888 5555
thehoxton.com

MONOCLE COMMENT: The
restaurant and bar, Lotti's, is
run by Soho House, meaning the
breakfast menu is tip-top and the
cocktails are stirred extra-strong.
It also cleverly conceals the
reception desk, which is hiding
beneath the stairs on the right.

2
212–231

⑤
Conservatorium Hotel, Oud-Zuid
Light touch

This neo-gothic building designed by Dutch architect Daniel Knuttel began life as a bank in 1897 and a century later was home to the Conservatorium van Amsterdam. When the music school outgrew it, the Set Hotels group bought the space and transformed it into a 129-room hotel.

Italian designer and architect Piero Lissoni has reinvigorated the historic building, with natural light playing a key part. The lobby and brasserie sit beneath a glass atrium, while many rooms benefit from the heritage-listed windows. Its closest neighbours are the city's most celebrated museums, including the Rijksmuseum, the Stedelijk and Van Gogh, as well as the lesser-known but still very much worthwhile Moco Museum.

27 Van Baerlestraat, 1071 AN
+ 31 (0)20 570 0000
conservatoriumhotel.com

MONOCLE COMMENT: Not only is there a gym (*see page 124*), a gin bar and a top restaurant led by Schilo Van Coevorden but also a luxury shopping gallery. Shops include Bonebakker jewellers, Skins Cosmetics and Meraki hair salon.

6

Sweets Hotel, citywide
Attractive spread

While traditional hotels may be housed in just one building, Sweets is spread across 28. "There is no hotel lobby with a receptionist and people get in using their phone," says artistic director Suzanne Oxenaar.

Rooms are dotted across the city in canal-side "bridge houses" that were originally built to shelter the operators of the locks upon which they sit. They were renovated by local architecture and design firm Space&Matter, which nimbly made the most of the little space available by using split levels and stowing drawers under beds where necessary. The final result is a collection of high-end yet cosy – or as the Dutch would say, *gezellig* – city boltholes.
+ 31 (0)20 740 1010
sweetshotel.amsterdam

Shop and stay
——
Amsterdam-based design company Droog has set up a one-bedroom hotel on the top floor of its shop (*see page 49*) and studio in Centrum. The space, which also includes a long, light-filled living area, is available to hire for small events as well.
droog.com

(7)
Maison Rika, Centrum
Boutique hideaway

In the heart of the De 9 Straatjes neighbourhood, one of the traditional 200-year-old corner houses has been converted into a pocket-sized guesthouse. Previously serving as a gallery, the space was acquired by Swedish fashion designer and former interior decorator Ulrika Lundgren in the hope of creating a cosy pied-à-terre. "People who come here don't want flashy five-star hotels: they're looking for something unique, something secret," she says.

Maison Rika only has two rooms, each of which occupies an entire floor and offers guests a panoramic view of the Herengracht canal. The house's ground floor delivers its fair share of distraction too: it simultaneously serves as a lobby, a concept boutique (*see page 54*) and a pop-up gallery. Although breakfast isn't included in the price, regular refreshments and a selection of small but tasty snacks are brought to the room during the day.

12 Oude Spiegelstraat, 1016 BM
+ 31 (0)20 330 1112
rikastudios.com

MONOCLE COMMENT: The free-of-charge concierge service will help you secure those hard-to-get restaurant reservations as well as tickets to the hottest shows. Guests can also pick up a copy of the in-house biannual publication *Rika Magazine*, with striking fashion pictorials and punchy articles.

Ⓑ
Hotel Okura, De Pijp
Tall storeys

Hotel Okura is an odd sight to behold: a 23-storey tower bordering the low-rise residential neighbourhood of De Pijp. The Japanese chain's only European outpost was designed by Dutch architect Bernard Bijvoet and opened in 1971.

A 10-minute cycle from the canal ring and an eight-minute taxi from the commercial district, it's well positioned for those in town on business. The 300 rooms are comfortable and decorated with dark-wood panelling and Japanese-inspired decor. Guests also have access to a lap pool, gym and sauna.
333 Ferdinand Bolstraat, 1072 LH
+31 (0)20 678 7111
okura.nl

MONOCLE COMMENT: Yamazato, the Michelin-starred restaurant on the ground floor, is one of Hotel Okura's four dining spots. Executive chef Masanori Tomikawa started as a porter in the hotel's Tokyo outpost before moving to Amsterdam to work in the kitchens in 1984. After training under Akira Oshima, Tomikawa took the reins. His *kaiseki* menu (a traditional Japanese multi-course affair) will impress any client.

Design hotels

A spate of new design hotels has shaken up the scene, targeting younger audiences with creative concepts and more affordable prices.

01 **Volkshotel, Oost:** This 172-room hotel opened in 2014 in the former offices of Dutch daily newspaper *De Volkskrant*. Evidence of this past life can be seen throughout the design, including photos from the city's counterculture.
volkshotel.nl

02 **Zoku, De Plantage:** This is more suited to young professionals who are either moving to the city or in town for a slightly longer period; its services include business-registration assistance and access to office equipment. The bar offers meeting rooms, co-working spaces and a fine wine menu.
livezoku.com

03 **Pension Homeland, Eastern Docklands:** The proximity to the harbour and various museums is the drawcard but the 1960s and 1970s-inspired interiors may be a little loud for some.
pensionhomeland.com

It's time for some dogged exploration

⑨
Lloyd Hotel & Cultural Embassy, Eastern Docklands
Come one, come all

It's a rather peculiar approach for a hotel to cater to all budgets under one roof but that's been Lloyd Hotel's concept since opening in 2004. "We wanted people to fit in and to be able to order breakfast in bed whether they were a one-star or five-star guest," says co-founder and artistic director Suzanne Oxenaar.

In its 100-year history the storied building, which is located in the old Eastern Docklands, has served as both a refugee and juvenile-detention centre, as well as an artists' studio. Top Dutch design talent such as MVRDV and Joep Van Lieshout worked to transform the existing spaces to accommodate 117 contemporary rooms, an expansive restaurant, a library and exhibition spaces for the in-house Cultural Embassy.
34 Oostelijke Handelskade, 1019 BN
+ 31 (0)20 561 3607
lloydhotel.com

MONOCLE COMMENT: Hotel guests are afforded free entry to the Cultural Embassy's busy calendar of events, which includes philosophy talks, modern-art exhibitions and annual Japanese market MonoJapan.

⑩
The Dylan, Centrum
Heritage hospitality

The Dylan is a dependable place to hang your hat while in town. Located on the canal ring in De 9 Straatjes, the five interjoining buildings operated as a charity from the 18th century; the original baker's ovens from the food bank line the walls of in-house French restaurant Vinkeles.

The privately owned hotel has 40 rooms, 16 of which were refurbished in 2014 by Dutch designer Remy Meijers. Our preference rests with the Scandi-simplicity of the five loft suites. Just watch your step as you weave between buildings: a condition of its heritage status means there are a few sudden floor changes.
384 Keizersgracht, 1016 GB
+ 31 (0)20 530 2010
dylanamsterdam.com

MONOCLE COMMENT: While the linens may be Italian, the plump beds are Dutch. Nilson mattresses will ensure a restful night's sleep.

(11)
W Hotel, Centrum
Bank on it

Two sister buildings just off Dam
Square mark W Hotel's first foray
onto the Dutch hotel scene. The
luxury chain planned to open
one 172-room hotel in the 1903
modernist telephone exchange
building but a happy accident saw
owner Liran Wizman also acquire
the old Kas Bank across the street.

While the handsome exteriors
of the Exchange might seem more
alluring, the stately feel of the
Bank's interior has clear appeal.
Its centrepiece is The Duchess
restaurant in the original banking
hall, with hand-painted floor tiles,
ornate wooden door frames and
a sweeping stained-glass roof.
Of the Bank's 66 rooms, 10 are
spacious suites. Furry friends are
also welcomed – and even catered
for on the room-service menus.
175 Spuistraat, 1012 VN
+31 (0)20 811 2500
wamsterdam.com

MONOCLE COMMENT: The benefits
of neighbouring buildings is the
roster of amenities available to
all guests. On the Exchange side is
a rooftop bar, plunge pool and
steak restaurant, while on the Bank
side is a gym, concept store (*see
pages 46 to 47*) and day spa hidden
behind a four-tonne vault door.

Grand Hotel Amrâth

On the border of Centrum and
the Eastern Docklands, not too
far from Centraal station, is the
gargantuan brick Grand Hotel
Amrâth. Heavily influenced
by art nouveau, it's an early
example of Amsterdam School;
architect Johan van der Mey
was commissioned by six
shipping companies in 1912 to
design a shared office building.
Its close proximity to the docks
allowed the companies to sell
tickets for voyages to the likes
of the Dutch East Indies.

Van der Mey wove nautical
motifs into the stained glass,
stonework, furniture and
finishings; the exterior features
a gallery of stone heads. It
opened as a five-star hotel in
2007 but the rooms are a tad
garish. The common areas are
open to the public.
amrathamsterdam.com

Food and drink
—— Going Dutch

Although the Dutch are known worldwide for their cheese, pancakes and apple pie, Amsterdam is not famed as a culinary destination. But if you know where to look, there's plenty going on in the city of canals.

Recent years have seen a huge shift from the exotic to the homegrown, with nearly all of the best restaurants now focusing on using seasonal, local ingredients from sustainable producers. This means menus that change regularly, inventive vegetarian cuisine despite the country's traditional obsession with meat, and modern Dutch fare that reinvents the old classics.

Very few locals live in the centre of Amsterdam so the best places are often a bit further afield. Amsterdammers love to eat out so hop on your bike and join them – but best to book ahead.

Restaurants
Chew on this

①
Buffet van Odette, Centrum
Bistro style

Odette Rigterink has had a clear vision ever since she started cooking food and selling it at a market in 1994: good meals made with good products, to be savoured and enjoyed. These days Buffet van Odette is a local institution famous for its truffle-cheese omelette, Frank's Smokehouse smoked salmon and sticky-toffee cake.

Its French-bistro style makes it perfect for a long, relaxed lunch accompanied by natural wine but you can also pop in for breakfast or call ahead to try the seasonal harissa mussels at dinner.
598 Prinsengracht, 1017 KS
+31 (0)20 423 6034
buffet-amsterdam.nl

Bar Spek, De Baarsjes
Leisurely lunches

Opening in time for breakfast and closing well after midnight, Bar Spek wants people to stay all day, making it a favourite among the young, freelance crowd in this increasingly vibrant part of town.

It's a low-key neighbourhood spot with an enormous menu that covers everything from overnight oats and eggs to pulled pork focaccia and truffle pizza – plus it's sat right on a canal, making it fantastic in summer. Drop by for a lazy lunch or check out the website for details of events, such as the popular gin-and-tonic nights.
1 Admiraal de Ruijterweg, 1057 JT
+31 (0)20 618 8102
barspek.nl

Guts & Glory, Centrum
Globetrotting cuisine

You know you're onto something unique when you enter Guts & Glory through its unusual exterior. Dutch chefs and best friends Guillaume de Beer and Freek van Noortwijk opened the restaurant with the idea of using every part of the animal, rotating the menu every three months.

The duo have now moved on to country-specific cuisines and the interior is always decorated to match. For all its fame this is an easygoing place, perfect for dinner with friends. Call a week ahead for weekend bookings.
6 Utrechtsestraat, 1017 VN
+31 (0)20 362 0030
gutsglory.nl

④

Worst Wijncafé, Westelijke Eilanden
Nice sausage

In a quiet part of town, this haunt
was set up as a way for owner Kees
Elfring (*pictured*) to bring quality
sausage to the city, something he
felt was lacking. Amsterdammers
clearly agreed with him because the
place is full every night with people
trying out the homemade selection,
such as the wild boar, the fennel
and the lobster.

The starter-sized servings are
ideal for sharing during a *borrel*
(evening drink) with friends. The
pigs' trotters – one of the few
imported ingredients – are highly
recommended.
171 Barentszstraat, 1013 NM
+31 (0)20 625 6167
dewerst.nl

⑤

Betty's, Rijnbuurt
Home comforts

Stepping into Betty's is a bit like
stepping into owners Gido and
Caroline Schweitzer's living room.
This homely vegetarian restaurant
has been a two-person operation
ever since it opened in 1988,
allowing the Schweitzers to create
a place where diners can stay all
night if they choose.

The three-course menu changes
every few weeks but one thing
you can expect is inventive food
packed with flavour that contains
influences from all over the world.
Betty's is an institution with a big
heart. Reservations are essential.
75 Rijnstraat, 1079 GX
+31 (0)20 644 5896
bettys.nl

⑥ Spang Makandra, De Pijp
Spice sensation

This tiny restaurant is always busy – and with good reason. The decor isn't particularly inspiring but the food is arguably the best Surinamese-Javanese food you can get in Amsterdam. Spang Makandra opened its doors in 1978 and remains a family business to this day. It is now run by son Budi Moestadja, who is usually on hand to provide recommendations.

It's a relaxed place and more often than not packed with regulars enjoying generous portions of roti with *pom* (a chicken and root-vegetable dish). Pop by for lunch and order the house special for a culinary tour through the former Dutch empire, comprising fried rice, noodles, chicken satay and Javanese *frikandel*, topped with a fried egg and a super-spicy potato sambal.
*39 Gerard Doustraat, 1072 VK
+31 (0)20 670 5081*

Potato pleasure

Vlaamse patat (Flemish-style chips) are almost a deity in the Netherlands. Hole-in-the-wall Vlaams Friteshuis Vleminckx has been serving golden cones of *patat* since 1957. For something different, try the satay sauce or *patatje oorlog*.
vleminckxdesausmeester.nl

⑦ Venus & Adonis, Jordaan
Rare discovery

If you're on the hunt for a juicy steak with some grilled tiger prawns, flawlessly seared scallops or, perhaps, a serving of lobster tail, look no further than Venus & Adonis. The meat is exclusively sourced from Dutch female Blonde d'Aquitaine cows for a more tasty and tender steak, and the restaurant makes good use of its charcoal grill.

The eclectic interior – think hexagonal hanging lights, yellow-suede chairs and a wooden ceiling – creates a comfortable and sophisticated ambiance.
*274 Prinsengracht, 1016 HH
+31 (0)20 421 1848
venusenadonis.nl*

⑧
Little Collins, De Pijp
Best of the brunch

Run by an Australian-Dutch couple, Little Collins channels that sunny Melbourne feeling with friendly staff and global flavours and influences. It gets busy at weekends so go during the week if possible.

The restaurant takes the now ubiquitous avo on toast to new levels with fennel, goat's cheese and dukkah; it also serves delicious waffles with English bacon or kimchi pancakes. In summer the outdoor terrace makes this place hard to beat.
*19F Eerste Sweelinckstraat, 1073 CL
+31 (0)20 753 9636
littlecollins.nl*

⑨
Scheepskameel, Eastern Docklands
Unfussy fine dining

The Scheepskameel experience begins with maître d' Bob, who greets you at the door like an old friend. "It should feel like coming home to your family," says head chef Tijs Jeurissen (*pictured*).

With its high ceilings and naval history, Scheepskameel (Ship's Camel) is not homely but it works. The dinner-only à la carte menu is European cooking that is suitable for all budgets and attracts a diverse clientele. Leave room: the madeleines are famously good.
*Gebouw 24, 7 Kattenburgerstraat,
1018 JA
+31 (0)20 337 9680
scheepskameel.nl*

10
NewWerktheater,
Eastern Docklands
Daring dining

Design agency Staat breathed
new life into this 1970s theatre by
transforming it into "a space for
everything we love", says creative
director Merel Korteweg. Though
grey on the outside, the interior is
anything but. Alongside a photo
studio and co-working space
you'll find a restaurant that drags
sleepy Amsterdammers out of bed
with hearty European breakfasts
– or pop in at lunchtime for
adventurous plates such as venison
croquettes. Eat dinner elsewhere:
the restaurant closes at 17.00.
*75 Oostenburgergracht, 1018 NC
+31 (0)20 572 1380
newwerktheater.com*

11
Pllek, Noord
Take me to the river

For a taste of the grittier north
take the free city ferry to this
restaurant-café constructed from
shipping containers on PllekBeach
along the IJ river. Grab a seat at the
shared tables and enjoy seasonal
fare such as mushrooms, steamed
mackerel or falafel.
 In summer this is a popular
place to soak up sunshine on the
deckchairs but its spacious interior
is also inviting in colder weather. It
hosts film screenings, yoga sessions
and music performances year-
round and is a family-friendly spot
that attracts a laid-back crowd.
*59 Tt. Neveritaweg, 1033 WB
+31 (0)20 290 0020
pllek.nl*

Must-try
Haring from Kras Haring
This delicacy of raw, salted
herring is best enjoyed in
a *broodje* (bread bun) with
crunchy onions and sweet
pickles at Kras Haring. The
herring here is from the
coveted catch known as
Hollandse nieuwe.
krasharing.nl

⑫
La Perla, Jordaan
Pizza perfection

Founded in Jordaan's charming "Little Italy" street, La Perla is a small corner restaurant that draws a mighty crowd. Most come for the pizza, which is packed with flavour, perfectly cooked and pleasingly irregular in shape. The menu only offers 11 types, with variations on the themes of cheese and pork featuring heavily.

Buffalo mozzarella is delivered fresh from Italy and everything is cooked in the wood-fuelled brick oven, making this one of the best pizza restaurants in the city. Takeaway is also available.
53 Tweede Tuindwarsstraat, 1015 RZ
+31 (0)20 624 8828
pizzaperla.nl

⑬
Wolf Atelier, Westelijke Eilanden
Rising above it all

Chef Michael Wolf's restaurant is the sort of place you go to impress someone – or treat yourself. The structure itself is striking: a mostly glass building that perches over the water on a 1920s industrial railway bridge. Upon entering the sleek grey-and-brass dining room you'll receive a welcome box with a mint, refreshing towel and bottle of filtered water. Lunchtime diners can enjoy six tartares in three sizes, while dinner is an inventive European menu of meat and fish. Try the 15-course tasting menu for a journey through Wolf's kitchen.
20 Westerdoksplein, 1013 AZ
+31 (0)20 344 6428
wolfatelier.nl

Fast and fried
───
Pronounced "fay-bo" and named after Ferdinand Bolstraat, the street where the chef learned his trade, Febo is a fast-food chain where you can get fried snacks from a vending machine. Popular choices include the *kipcorn* chicken stick and *frikadel* sausage.
febo.nl

⑭ Bak, Westelijke Eilanden
Room with a view

Despite beginning life as a pop-up, Bak has become a much-celebrated mainstay since opening in 2012. Its menu centres around top-quality regional produce and the chefs only use meat and fish caught in the wild. With at least 500 natural wines available, including the increasingly popular orange variety, it may well have one of the largest collections in the country.

Situated in a former warehouse, the whitewashed room enables diners to enjoy the view across the old harbour and the IJ river in an elegant setting.
468 Van Diemenstraat, 1013 CR
+31 (0)20 737 2553
bakrestaurant.nl

⑮ Sama Sebo, Oud-Zuid
Indonesian feast

When Daniel Woldringh opened Sama Sebo in 1969 he had no idea that his restaurant would become a cornerstone of Amsterdam's popular Indonesian food scene. Decades later the 1970s interior still charms, with copper pots and pans hanging from the low ceiling and a wooden bar to perch at.

The main event is the *rijsttafel* (rice table), a spectacular spread of more than 20 small sharing dishes such as beef rendang, chicken satay and tiger prawns.
27 Pieter Cornelisz Hooftstraat,
1071 BL
+31 (0)20 662 8146
samasebo.nl

⑯ Moak Pancakes, Oud-West
Go flat out

Pancakes may be a national dish but Moak isn't doing things the traditional way. Opened in 2016 by Sten van den Bedem and Sammy Salimian as an experiment in healthy US-style pancakes, it has become a much-loved gem.

Made with spelt flour, buttermilk and eggs (vegan options are also available), these thick, fluffy delights are served three-in-a-pile with anything from bacon and maple syrup to peanut butter and fruit. Throw in juice and sofas and this becomes an infallible brunch spot.
34H De Clercqstraat, 1052 NG
+31 (0)20 334 6995
moakpancakes.nl

Sharing dishes?
I'm not familiar
with that concept

⑱
De Japanner, De Pijp
Late-night bites

Modelled on a Japanese *izakaya* (gastropub for after-work drinks), De Japanner hits the sweet spot between restaurant and bar. The small menu features Japanese dishes with local seafood, such as herring sashimi, and *izakaya* classics such as *agedashidofu* (deep-fried tofu), all perfect for washing down with Japanese whiskey, saké or even a bottle of Tokyo craft beer.

It's walk-in only from 19.00, giving the place an informal feel. Plus, unusually for Amsterdam, the kitchen doesn't close until the front door does; 03.00 at the weekend.
228 Albert Cuypstraat, 1073 BN
+31 (0)20 233 9939
dejapanner.com

⑰
Festina Lente, Jordaan
Canal-side lunch spot

Beloved by locals, this living room-style café is all about taking a second to catch your breath in an increasingly hectic world. A café has been here in one form or another for more than a century and this iteration has been popular for lunch breaks and post-work drinks ever since it opened in 1998.

Think healthy and inexpensive soups, salads and sandwiches in a homely wooden interior complete with squishy sofas and shelves of books. Come summer, grab a table outside on the pretty Looiersgracht and watch canal life pass by.
40B Looiersgracht, 1016 VS
+31 (0)20 638 1412
cafefestinalente.nl

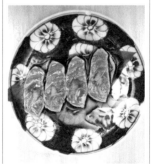

⑲
D'Vijff Vlieghen, Centrum
Culinary museum

Although D'Vijff Vlieghen (Five Flies) opened its doors in 1939, the dazzling interior – with its antique glassware, tiles, prints and wooden beams – feels centuries older. Five themed rooms provide plenty of snug spots that belie the restaurant's size (270 covers excluding the private areas).

Ask for a tour if it's quiet to see the Rembrandt etchings and Walt Disney drawing in the guestbook. The menu is modern Dutch, featuring the likes of tuna steak baked in *speculaas* spices and ice cream with herbs.
294-302 Spuistraat, 1012 VX
+31 (0)20 530 4060
vijffvlieghen.nl

⑳ John Dory, Centrum
Catch of the day

John Dory is all about regional seafood prepared in exciting ways. The restaurant is spread across two floors of a 17th-century former canal-side warehouse: there's a small bar for oysters and wine downstairs and a more formal fish restaurant upstairs.

Lights suspended from fishing rope and wooden beams make this a cosy dinner spot for those seeking a taste of old-world Amsterdam. The menu changes daily according to the catch from the North Sea but don't miss the red mullet if it's available – it's the owner's favourite.

999 Prinsengracht, 1017 KM
+31 (0)20 622 9044
johndory.nl

㉑ De Kas, Watergraafsmeer
Garden party

It doesn't get any fresher than eating food grown in a restaurant's own garden. Located in the stately Frankendael Park, De Kas and its nursery occupy old municipal greenhouses renovated by Dutch designer Piet Boon (restaurants in greenhouses are somewhat of a trend in the city, perhaps in an attempt to maximise light during the moody winter months).

The uncomplicated, vegetable-oriented menu changes daily depending on what's harvested and includes meat, fish and dairy products.

3 Kamerlingh Onneslaan, 1097 DE
+31 (0)20 462 4562
restaurant.dekas.nl

㉒
Choux, Centrum
Conversation starter

You'd be hard pressed to guess that Choux's smart address inside Spring House – a multidisciplinary space for creatives – used to be the site of a distillery on a street known for prostitution and depravity. These days the restaurant attracts a different professional crowd.

Owners Figo van Onna and Merijn van Berlo experiment with umami-loaded sustainable ingredients such as seaweed to get people thinking about meat-free cooking. The results are impressive, particularly when enjoyed with a specially paired glass of natural wine.
128 De Ruijterkade, 1011 AC
+31 (0)61 651 2364
choux.nl

㉔
Wilde Zwijnen, Indische Buurt
Far from a boar

Wilde Zwijnen was one of the first upmarket restaurants to open in up-and-coming Indische Buurt back in 2010 and its modern take on Dutch food has helped draw interest to the area. Expect regional vegetables prepared in inventive ways alongside fresh seafood and make sure you try the eponymous wild boar if available.

The restaurant has an intimate feel, even if it's full. For a more speedy meal drop into the adjoining Eetcafé and feast on tapas-inspired bites such as cod chips and aubergine cream.
23 Javaplein, 1095 CJ
+31 (0)20 463 3043
wildezwijnen.com

㉓
Entrepot, Centrum
On fire

Housed in an 18th-century warehouse on the Entrepotdok canal, this restaurant has been drawing in diners since 2017. Chef Arvid Schmidt's mouthwatering menus change daily and feature dishes such as roasted beef neck and salt-crusted yellow beetroot, all made with seasonal produce.

The interior is decked out with Dutch designer Friso Kramer's Revolt chairs and cosily lit by hanging pendant lamps that hover between chunky wooden beams. Nab a seat facing the kitchen.
7–8 Entrepotdok, 1018 AD
+31 (0)20 341 5722
restaurantentrepot.nl

Coffee
Bean counters

 Vuurtoreneiland, Eastern Docklands
Island adventure

It may take some effort (reservations are recommended a month in advance) but Vuurtoreneiland is worth it. The experience starts with a ferry ride to Lighthouse Island, a Unesco World Heritage site, on IJmeer Lake. In winter guests dine in a 19th-century fort; in summer the feast moves to a greenhouse to maximise the view. The European set menu focuses on food prepared using traditional techniques: think sheep's cheese, buck meat and wild garlic.
Boats depart from opposite Lloyd Hotel, 34 Oostelijke Handelskade, 1019 BN
+31 (0)20 362 1664
vuurtoreneiland.nl

① **Lot Sixty One, Oud-West**
Much-loved micro-roastery

Because they roast on-site, the air at Lot Sixty One is always heavy with the scent of coffee: rich and earthy with a hint of chocolate. The menu focuses on beans from small farms such as Finca Toño in Costa Rica's West Valley and changes seasonally according to the harvest.

This is a great place to grab a velvety-black espresso when en route to the nearby shops at De Hallen. But it's also equally suited to hunkering down with a cappuccino, a pastry and a book for an hour or two.
112 Kinkerstraat, 1053 ED
+31 (0)61 605 4227
lotsixtyonecoffee.com

(2)
Scandinavian Embassy, De Pijp
World view

The Argentinean-Swedish-Polish team behind this shop are serious about coffee. Their weekly changing menu specialises in filter coffee and they buy everything from a network of roasteries across Scandinavia, which source beans from all over the world.

But this place isn't just about espresso. The owners are on a mission to explore the coffee plant's full potential, serving coffee-flower tea and even coffee-pickled oysters. They also have a few Scandi treats, including meatballs, øllebrød (beer-and-bread porridge) and rye bread.

34 Sarphatipark, 1072 PB
+31 (0)61 951 8199
scandinavianembassy.nl

(3)
The Coffee District, Oud-Zuid
Beans around town

This peaceful spot in leafy Oud-Zuid has large windows overlooking the picturesque Hendrik Jacobszstraat that flood the coffee shop with natural light. Opened by husband-and-wife duo Adil and Rosa Loukane in 2019, The Coffee District serves smooth coffee made using beans from Amsterdam's Lot Sixty One roastery. And don't miss the fine selection of homemade sweet treats (we'd recommend the coconut macaroons and sea-salt chocolate-chip cookies).

The spacious, whitewashed premises doubles as a shop selling everything you need to make the perfect coffee in the comfort of your own home, from pots by Japanese brand Kinto to flasks by Australia's Huskee.

18 Hendrik Jacobszstraat, 1075 PD
+31 (0)64 820 0518
coffeedistrict.nl

Must-try
Apple pie at Café Papeneiland
This dessert has been a favourite with the Dutch since the Middle Ages. This version is homemade, unfussy and famous (Bill Clinton stopped by for a taste), with a golden-brown crust and layers of moist apples.
+31 (0)20 624 1989

(4)
Toki, Jordaan
Easy does it

This light-filled hangout offers a superb range of coffee from Berlin roastery Bonanza, with an ever-changing selection of beans. Order a flat white and a slice of fresh lemon-drizzle cake and sink into the large sofa along with the rest of the neighbourhood. This is a place to take it easy.

Owner Jeff Flink (*pictured, on left*) has also created a brew bar for his Bellocq tea menu, key for the perfect cup of Lapsang Souchong or Alpine herbal blend *pic du midi*. For something harder there's a fridge full of half-litre beers.
15 Binnen Dommerssstraat, 1013 HK
+31 (0)20 363 6009
tokiho.amsterdam

Baked goods

01 **Hartog's Volkoren Bakkerij en Maalderij, Oost:** The Hartog family's wholemeal loaves have been drawing queues of people for more than a century. Try the sunflower-seed bread for extra crunch or the *gevulde koeken* (almond cookies) for a traditional Dutch snack.
volkorenbrood.nl

02 **Bakken met Passie, De Pijp:** After visiting Albert Cuypmarkt (*see page 41*), drop into this café for a rest and a bite to eat. Its croissants, cooked the French way, are buttery, flaky perfection.
bakkenmetpassie.nl

03 **De Laatste Kruimel, Centrum:** Every last crumb tends to disappear at this much-loved bolthole in the centre of town. It's more of a takeaway place so grab a slice of freshly baked quiche or order a piping hot toastie and eat it by the canal.
delaatstekruimel.nl

Food markets and retailers
Gourmets galore

① Fromagerie Abraham Kef, Jordaan
Speciality cheese

You can't cross a canal without running into a cheese shop in Amsterdam but Kef is one of a kind. There's plenty of top-notch French fromage but go for the Dutch *kaas* (cheese). Even though the selection is small it's from the country's best producers, and the staff will happily talk you through the range.

Since 2000, owner Marike van der Werff (*pictured*) has been handpicking whatever she likes each season and selling it alongside delicious fig bread, pâté and pickles. Book a month in advance for the Sunday tasting sessions.
192B Marnixstraat, 1016 TJ
+31 (0)20 420 0097
abrahamkef.nl

② De Pasteibakkerij, Rijnbuurt
Meat-lovers' paradise

Floris Brester and Diny Schouten (*both pictured*) are determined to revive the Netherlands' charcuterie tradition, using parts of animals – mainly Dutch pigs – that are often overlooked. As well as terrines, rillettes and pâtés made with anything from pigs' trotters to "pest" geese culled at Schiphol Airport, they also sell white pudding, sausages and smoked calf's tongue, among other things.

The pair smoke everything in their tiny shop, which is tucked away on a quiet street and only open on Fridays and Saturdays.
2 Hoendiepstraat, 1079 LT
+31 (0)65 347 5512
depasteibakkerij.nl

(3)

Noordermarkt, Jordaan
Farmers' market

Every Saturday the Noordermarkt's large food section opens to the public. Bustling with people who come from far and wide, this is a great place to grab some fresh, seasonal produce.

It's a one-stop shop for the ultimate picnic or dinner party: truffle ravioli, raw-milk butter, juicy dates, colourful displays of vegetables, fresh oysters, Dutch cheese, fragrant herbs – and everything is organic. There's also an adjoining flea market on Mondays where you can pick up antique sunglasses, rare books, old records and other curiosities.
Noordermarkt, 1015 MV
noordermarkt-amsterdam.nl

(4)

Foodhallen, Oud-West
The spice of life

Foodhallen food market is the star attraction in the cleverly renovated De Hallen complex. It isn't huge but the market is bordered by stalls serving everything from prawn-tempura buns to raw salad bowls, and there are shared tables dotted through the centre.

Kick a hangover with a sausage, bacon and chip roll from Bulls and Dogs, go healthy with *goi cuon* rice-paper rolls from Viet View or try Le Big Fish's Dutch *kibbeling* (battered fried fish). Come for a weekday lunch to beat the crowds and don't miss the gin-and-tonic bar.
51 Bellamyplein, 1053 AT
+31 (0)62 926 5037
foodhallen.nl

Must-try
Bitterballen at Café de Pels
Bitterballen are the centrepiece of any Dutch evening gathering (known as a *borrel*) and with good reason. Hidden inside the crunchy, golden exterior of these deep-fried balls is a rich, gooey roux flecked with meat. Dip them in some sharp mustard for the full effect. Veal *bitterballen* from Holtkamp are among the best and the elegant Café de Pels, which dates back to the 1960s, is a great place to enjoy them.

Other traditional *borrelhapjes* (*borrel* snacks) to enjoy with a drink include *garnelenkroketten* (prawn croquettes) and *ossenworst* (raw beef sausage). Or try the *borrelbord*, featuring top-notch terrine from De Pasteibakkerij (*see page 40*).
cafedepels.nl

Drinks
Wet your whistle

⑤
Thull's, Oost
Pickles and preserves

The first thing you notice is the smell of vinegar. Thull's specialises in all things fermented, pickled and preserved, from jams and gherkins to sardines. It was set up in 2015 by Simone van Thull to share her love of "healthy and colourful" food.

The shop also has a café where you can grab bites such as a smoked trout, pickled fennel and cress sandwich. Make sure you try the most popular product: water kefir. This gut-repairing, gently sparkling punch is produced by mixing water, water kefir grains, dried figs, lemon and sugar.
69 Pretoriusstraat, 1092 GB
+31 (0)20 363 5474
thulls.nl

①
Café-Restaurant de Plantage,
De Plantage
Birdwatching in style

This soaring conservatory next to the historic Artis Zoo is a great spot for a drink. In the summer one side opens onto a tree-lined square where you can watch tropical birds strutting and preening.

The crowd here is smart, making it a foolproof option for drinks with clients in the week. The extensive wine list is organised by taste – bright and elegant or earthy and spicy – and there are eight different gins. Bar snacks such as oysters and pork belly are available when you get peckish.
36 Plantage Kerklaan, 1018 CZ
+31 (0)20 760 6800
caferestaurantdeplantage.nl

(2)
The Blue Tea House, Oud-Zuid
Tipples on a terrace

As soon as the sun comes out, Amsterdammers flock to the terraces of this modernist pavilion to soak up the rays with a beer in hand. Built in 1937, in 2019 it came under the stewardship of brewers Brouwerij 't IJ, who hired Amsterdam's Studio Modijefsky to work on its redesign.

The outdoor terrace has been given a facelift with plenty of seating, parasols and twinkly lights. Pale ales and small-batch beers are served at the wooden bar; the 't Blauwe Theehuis pils, in particular, is worth trying.
5 Vondelpark, 1071 AA
+31 (0)20 235 7170
brouwerijhetij.nl

(3)
Pont 13, Houthavens
All aboard

Built in 1927, this boat spent most of the 20th century ferrying people across the IJ but is now anchored to the remote (by Amsterdam standards) Haparandadam jetty. It's worth the journey: the views are spectacular and the isolated location makes this place feel undiscovered.

The industrial interior retains many of the boat's original features and the benches on the top deck are a great place to enjoy a beer. For food, order the oysters or a burger. Private events are common so phone to check opening times.
50 Haparandadam, 1013 AT
+31 (0)20 770 2722
pont13.nl

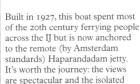

If you eat any more chips you won't be able to take off

⑤

GlouGlou, De Pijp
Down-to-earth wine bar

GlouGlou is out to prove that
Amsterdam is not just about beer.
The bar serves only natural wine,
mainly from Europe, and the staff
are happy to advise. With nearly
everything available by the glass,
you can experiment without
breaking the bank.

The pub-style interior and
unpretentious approach make
this a far cry from conventional
wine bars. Throw in snails, cheese
boards and fresh bread and you
can see why it's a favourite among
the De Pijp crowd. There is also a
wine shop for takeaways.
3 Tweede van der Helststraat, 1073 AE
+31 (0)20 233 8642
glouglou.nl

④

Wynand Fockink, Centrum
High spirits

Before gin there was *genever*.
Wynand Fockink serves the
juniper-flavoured liqueur, also
known as Dutch gin, the old-
fashioned way: in a tulip glass filled
all the way to the top, so you have
to bow to take your first sip.

The lively bar is a *proeflokaal*, or
tasting room that dates back to the
17th century, as do the adjoining
shop and distillery. The owners
produce more than 70 liqueurs,
including *Hansje in de Kelder* (Little
Hans in the Basement), a celebratory
drink tinged with apricot, lemon,
orange and cinnamon.
31 Pijlsteeg, 1012 HH
+31 (0)20 639 2695
wynand-fockink.nl

Complex flavours
—
If you like your craft beer with
oomph, don't miss Oedipus's
creative range with delights
such as Thai Thai, a tipple with
Asian spices. The brewery,
off the beaten track in Noord,
also serves delicious burgers
and makes a great lazy-
afternoon destination.
oedipus.com

⑦
Kanarie Club, Oud-West
Chirpy vibe

Kanarie Club sits at the end of the Foodhallen (*see page 41*) inside the city's former tram depot. By day it's a relaxed café but at night the space comes into its own. Join the trendy Oud-West crowd with an expertly mixed cocktail and sit in a cosy cubbyhole on industrial bar stools by the old tram tracks, or up in the raised swimming pool area. No swimming suits are required: the empty pool is a relic from the building's past when squatters used it to gather rainwater. The bright interior is by design powerhouse Studio Modijefsky.
51 Bellamyplein, 1053 AT
+31 (0)20 218 1775
kanarieclub.nl

⑥
Café Welling, Oud-Zuid
Arty party

Bruine cafés – so called due to their cosy wooden interiors and nicotine-stained ceilings – are an intrinsic part of Amsterdam life. Café Welling is one of the most charming examples of these shrines to the Dutch idea of *gezelligheid* (*see pages 75 to 76*). A favourite among writers and artists, perhaps because of its location within earshot of the wonderful Het Concertgebouw concert hall (*see page 99*), this small but atmospheric place is a snug spot for a few early-evening (or late-night) beers or some *genever* with the locals. Portraits of famed intellectual clientele past and present line the walls.

Food at Café Welling is traditional pub-snack fare – think basic cheese toasties and boiled eggs – and live jazz concerts are often held here.
32 Jan Willem Brouwersstraat,
1071 LN
+31 (0)20 662 0155
cafewelling.nl

On the tiles

01 De School, De Baarsjes: Housed in an old technical school, De School's nightclub has a capacity of 700 and focuses on Amsterdam DJs. With a gym, concert space, café and restaurant, the complex is open 24 hours at weekends (*see page 97*).
deschoolamsterdam.nl

02 Warehouse Elementenstraat, Nieuwe-West: Famous for raves in the 1990s, this warehouse has recently reopened, giving up to 2,500 people the chance to party to house, techno and electro in a historic club.
elementenstraat.nl

03 De Marktkantine, Westerpark: This venue dates back to 1936 and has hosted many live music and theatre events. It has been in its current club-gallery-restaurant incarnation since 2014 and has a range of rooms that provide plenty of scope for a colourful night out.
marktkantine.nl

04 Undercurrent, Noord: Located in the cutting-edge NDSM complex, Undercurrent hosts house and techno parties and boasts great views of the city from its floating platform in the north of IJ harbour. It also has an outdoor terrace extending onto the water.
undercurrent.nl

05 Shelter, Noord: Modelling itself as a Berlin-style club, this industrial-chic underground venue north of the river is a popular spot for techno, house and other dance music.
shelteramsterdam.nl

Retail
—— Fill your tote

Innovative retailers are prospering across Amsterdam's streets and the historical architecture of this fine old city, from heritage banks to canal-front houses, is being reimagined as their playground.

The best businesses here enjoy a global customer mix, which enables entrepreneurs to apply fresh approaches to bricks-and-mortar shopping. It also doesn't hurt that the Dutch are a tasteful bunch. From smart buyers with an eye for the most offbeat fashion to potters crafting quirky ceramics, a quality retail niche has been carved out.

Vintage treasures and new designs are waiting to be discovered here so use these pages as a guide for your jaunt around the city's streets and markets. Fill your tote with everything from books to brogues – and a good bunch of flowers – to brighten your day.

Concept stores
Mixed retail

①
X Bank, Centrum
Going Dutch

Inside the design-savvy heritage Kas Bank building in Amsterdam's centre, X Bank provides an engulfing space for those who appreciate great products and thoughtful design. Its abiding mission is to highlight design and fashion brands with distinctly Dutch roots.

From cedar-infused gin made in Schiedam to Jackie Villevoye's hand-embroidered collection, there are plenty of Dutch goods to fill your suitcase.
172 Spuistraat, 1012 VT
+ 31 (0)20 811 3320
xbank.amsterdam

2

Hutspot, De Pijp
Creative gathering

Named after a traditional Dutch stew, Hutspot is a melting pot of creative talent and promising labels from Amsterdam through to northern Scandinavia. Pick up breezy summer items from Stieglitz or beautiful photos on pinewood by StigerWoods.

It's staffed by an enthusiastic team who are happy to inform you of book launches and in-store events, and if you're tired of shopping there is a barber on hand. There are also locations on Rozengracht and in the Magna Plaza shopping centre.
4 Van Woustraat, 1073 LL
+31 (0)20 223 1331
hutspot.com

I'm calling this more the trolley dachshund

③
Concrete Matter, Centrum
In the bag

"What looks beautiful should
be produced in a beautiful way,"
says Concrete Matter's co-founder
Jacob Garvelink. The timber-
lined space reflects his good
taste and the ambitions of the
brand, which caters to men with
adventurous spirits.

Everything here is durable and
timeless, from Merz B Schwanen
shirts to kitchenware from French
pocket-knife maker Opinel. Visitors
who wish to stock up can take
advantage of international shipping
for bigger pieces or bulk purchases
for their next adventure.
12 Gasthuismolensteeg, 1016 AN
+ 31 (0)20 261 0933
concrete-matter.com

④
The Otherist, Centrum
Curiouser and curiouser

Inspired by renaissance
wunderkammers (cabinets of
curiosity), The Otherist has been
selling trinkets and treasures
since 2006. From taxidermy to
cardboard creations, the quirky
melange of objects reflects the
soul of the founders.

"The Otherist is our idea
of the world, a microcosm of
who we are," says co-founder
Joshua Walters. If you're up
for a trip down the rabbit hole
and have a soft spot for peculiar
items, you might never leave.
6 Leliegracht, 1015 DE
+ 31 (0)20 320 0420
otherist.com

Ⓢ
Droog, Centrum
All under one roof

This monumental building, which once housed Amsterdam's textile guild, accommodates a variety of sharply designed spaces. Inside you'll find an exhibition gallery, a concept store, a lush garden and a breezy café, all under the auspices of Dutch design company Droog.

The shop stocks everything from iconic Dutch designers such as Marcel Wanders to emerging labels such as Afriek. On the top floor there is also the one-bedroom Hôtel Droog, a bright and airy suite filled, naturally, with Dutch design.

7B Staalstraat, 1011 JJ
+ 31 (0)20 523 5059
droog.com

⑥
Restored, Jordaan
Take it easy

Those searching for a keepsake with a clean aesthetic and a good story should look no further than Restored. This pared-down shop stocks plenty of trophies for your home, whether you're into ceramics, quality magazines or textiles from small labels.

Restored stocks minimalist brands such as Royal Republiq for leather goods and Monokel for sunglasses, as well as its own label, which does a smart wireframe plant holder in collaboration with Spitsberg. You'll feel serene and, well, restored after browsing this lovely space.

39 Haarlemmerdijk, 1013 KA
+ 31 (0)20 337 6473
restored.nl

❶
ETQ Store, Centrum
Minimalistic designs

ETQ's cavernous two-storey space is an ambitious statement from the minimalist men's footwear brand. The label has enjoyed rapid global success since launching in 2010 and no penny has been spared on forming a flagship to match its global prowess.

Designed by Amsterdam's Studio Jos van Dijk, the sprawling polished concrete and raw metal trimmings have transformed a former nightclub into a slick cave for shoes and clothes. The low-cut leather trainers that ETQ is renowned for can be found here but so too can a tight selection of international brands, including Études and Harmony.
465 Singel, 1012 WP
+ 31 (0)20 261 3815
etqstore.com

②
Afura, Oud-West
Simple pleasures

Victor ter Hark and Len Koster founded online menswear shop Afura in 2011 and opened this bricks-and-mortar outpost in 2016. The residential neighbourhood may seem an unconventional choice but, flanked by good cafés and inspiring architecture, it's worth the trip.

"We're not a high street shop, our brands don't suit that," says Koster, noting that Afura is the only place in the Netherlands that sells some of the labels stocked here, such as Italian technical outerwear brand Aspesi and offerings from Japan and the US.
164 Jan Pieter Heijestraat, 1054 MI.
+ 31 (0)20 331 3091
afurastore.com

③

No Label, Oud-Zuid
Tailor-made

No Label aims to take the fuss out of the men's clothes-shopping experience, leaving just well-made, good-fitting fashion. The formula is showcased at the brand's flagship store in the retail district in Amsterdam's south. Here well-appointed staff guide customers to tastefully toned knitwear, classically cut slim suits and a selection of relaxed footwear with prices that are pleasingly friendly on the wallet. For those with a little more time on their hands, No Label also offers a comprehensive tailoring service.
66 Willemsparkweg, 1071 HK
+ 31 (0)20 846 5591
nolabel.nl

④
Cowboys 2 Catwalk, Centrum
Prêt à porter

Cowboys 2 Catwalk rode into town
as Amsterdam's exclusive stockist
of Comme des Garçons Play in
2006. The shop has grown and
today strong Belgian designers,
including Dries Van Noten, sit
well with Japanese labels.

The shop's buyers have also
introduced newer labels to the
city, including Russia's subversive
Gosha Rubchinskiy. Cowboys 2
Catwalk is smartly divided into
three distinct sections with a
transparent glass floor, which
offers shoppers sweeping views
of the brands below.
107 Utrechtsestraat, 1017 VL
+ 31 (0)20 623 9694
cowboys2catwalk.com

Mixed fashion
His and hers

①
We Are Labels, Centrum
Bank on it

When Pieter-Bas Broeke opened the
first We Are Labels shop in 2010, it
was in reaction to the city's lack of
retailers showcasing independent
designers. "The Netherlands was
dominated by jeans stores carrying
all the same brands," says Broeke,
"so we started our first boutique
with 10 small labels."

The shop now has six outposts
across the city, the most impressive
of which is housed in a former bank
on Raadhuisstraat. Here you can
find Swedish coat-makers Elvine,
Amsterdam-based Club Manhattan
and in-house brand Another-Label.
46-50 Raadhuisstraat, 1016 DG
+ 31 (0)20 331 3850
wearelabels.com

2
Teym, Centrum
No-nonsense necessities

Teym is a brand that has forged
its identity on structured clothing.
The products are overseen by
founder and designer Maxime
Cartens (*pictured, on left*) and
include parkas designed to endure
cold winters, as well as Italian
leather bags.

Cartens, who has worked with
Karl Lagerfeld and H&M, says she
strives to produce clothes in an
ethical manner. Her slower pace
and careful approach have gained a
dedicated (and patient) following.
*17HS Iepenplein, 1091 JN
+ 31 (0)20 261 3876
teym.eu*

3
Margriet Nannings, Centrum
Laid-back browsing

Designer Margriet Nannings has
built a mini shopping empire on
the Prinsenstraat: one shop for
women, one for men and even
an outlet for bargain hunters.

The neighbouring shops are
an extension of her personality. "I
care for quality and unique designs
but the colours and styles of other
brands should complement each
other as well," says Nannings. That
down-to-earth nature is apparent
in the labels she stocks, including
APC, Comme des Garçons, Maison
Margiela and her own wares.
*6, 8 & 15 Prinsenstraat, 1015 DC
Women: + 31 (0)20 620 7672
Men: + 31 (0)20 620 3413
margrietnanningswebshop.com*

4
Ennu, Oud-Zuid
Where fashion meets passion

High-end fashion for men and
women sits comfortably in this
lavishly designed retailer just off
Van Breestraat, a street for luxury
shopping that you'll find next to
Vondelpark.

Expect fresh-off-the-runway
looks from the world's best and
most avant garde fashion designers.
Owner and buyer Pieter Baane's
knack for trailblazing comes across
in a retail design that never fails to
surprise, with sprightly art pieces
that adorn its vibrant green walls.
*15 Cornelis Schuytstraat, 1071 JC
+ 31 (0)20 673 5265
ennu.nl*

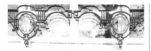

Womenswear
Wardrobe essentials

① Rika Studio, Centrum
Fashion polymath

Swedish designer Ulrika Lundgren leads a busy life. A glimpse into it can be had in this charming corner of the Herengracht canal and Oude Spiegelstraat, where Lundgren operates a hotel (*see page 22*), a lifestyle shop and her womenswear label Rika Studio. Her designs tend to balance Scandinavian refinement with bright colours.

Visitors can also grab a copy of *Rika Magazine*, in which editorials showcase the designer's fine work as well as pieces from her favourite brands and photographers.
9 Oude Spiegelstraat, 1016 BM
+ 31 (0)20 330 1112
rikastudios.com

⑤ Verse, Centrum
Sustainable shopping

Style and sustainability go hand in hand at Verse. Stocking everything from rain jackets made from recycled bottles to fair trade alpaca scarves, the shop sells the best and brightest in environmentally conscious fashion and beauty from around the world.

"I started Verse in 2016 after working for more than a decade in the commercial fashion industry," says founder and CEO Ciara Shah. "I wanted to take my knowledge and create the first sustainability-led concept store." There's now a second space in De Pijp.
581-1 Prinsengracht, 1016 HT
+ 31 (0)65 200 1410
versegoodstore.com

In good taste

Vanilia is arguably one of Amsterdam's most successful womenswear brands. Its on-trend cuts are made in a socially responsible manner and its approach to physical shops is equally noble, repurposing heritage buildings in a sensitive fashion.
vanilia.com

2

Maha, Centrum
Street smarts

This shop takes a novel approach to women's fashion: stock includes feminine streetwear and smaller-sized menswear items. "We started because I was always wearing my boyfriend's clothes as I couldn't buy what I wanted in Amsterdam," says Saskia van Hofwegen, who launched Maha with her boyfriend Dian Iskandar (*both pictured*) in 2015.

With women open to more masculine silhouettes, the shop quickly gained a cult following. Expect to find the latest from Opening Ceremony and Adidas.
105 Vijzelstraat, 1017 HH
+ 31 (0)20 363 5561
shop.maha-amsterdam.com

1

Keramiek Atelier Marjoke de Heer, Noord
Seamless ceramics

On the outskirts of Noord lies Keramiek Atelier Marjoke de Heer, which was established in 1994. The ceramics collection consists of pieces that are "one of a kind and, above all, made by the same pair of hands," says owner Marjoke de Heer.

Her ceramics are finished with self-developed glazes inspired by ancient Asian traditions. Celadon, Shino, flambé glaze and Temmoku are some of her signature styles. Her beautifully crafted tableware, garden objects and pots range from €10 to €1,000.
243 Schellingwouderdijk, 1023 NG
+ 31 (0)20 490 4936
marjokedeheer.com

2
Frozen Fountain, Centrum
Splash of colour

The best of Dutch design is to be
found at Frozen Fountain. Working
in close collaboration with art
schools across The Netherlands
and further afield means that it's
a hotbed for emerging talent and
has fostered the likes of Marcel
Wanders and Piet Hein Eek.

First opened in 1985, the shop
moved to its picturesque location
on the Prinsengracht canal in 1992.
Today it stocks a colourful array
of homeware and furniture from
international brands such as Cassina
and Zanotta as well as homegrown
talent including Paul Heijnen.
645 Prinsengracht, 1016 HV
+ 31 (0)20 622 9375
frozenfountain.nl

3
Moooi, Jordaan
Throw some shapes

Moooi specialises in lighting,
furniture and textiles, finishing
most of its pieces with a flamboyant
touch. If you're not afraid of colour
and appreciate humorous design,
make sure you swing by.

The firm, founded in 2001
by Marcel Wanders and Casper
Vissers, exudes avant gardism
and boldness. The duo enjoy
blowing up proportions and
putting their twist on traditional
products. Brands such as Front,
Studio Job and Arihiro Miyake
are sold alongside Moooi's in-
house creations.
187 Westerstraat, 1015 MA
+ 31 (0)20 528 7760
moooi.com

④ Gastronomie Nostalgie, Centrum
Treasure chest

The selection of vintage artefacts in this jam-packed shop is astonishingly diverse – and with price tags to match. Many of the antique items, such as silver candlesticks and porcelain, were originally owned by wealthy Europeans or legendary hotels.

Owner Andre Duijves says he scours international auctions for antique china, glassware and more. "I believe that table decorations are like jewellery for your home," says Duijves, who has an eye for crystal carafes, finely finished whiskey glasses and silver napkin rings.
304 Nieuwezijds Voorburgwal, 1012 RV
+ 31 (0)20 422 6226
gastronomienostalgie.nl

Three more denim emporiums

01 **Mick Keus, Centrum:**
Mick Keus unites the
old with the new by
customising vintage
Levi 501s. Each pair is
unique; just pop in and
find your size.
mickkeus.nl

02 **Denim City, Oud-West:**
Among the city's many
denim-driven concepts,
Denim City is a whole new
breed. On weekdays it's
an innovation centre,
archive and workplace; at
the weekend it's a shop
with a tailor who adjusts
your denim on the fly.
denimcity.org

03 **Denham, Oud-Zuid:** This
international brand was
founded in Amsterdam
and its flagship store
stocks myriad styles.
denhamthejeanmaker.com

①
Tenue de Nîmes, Jordaan
Distinctive denim

Tenue de Nîmes, the go-to jeans
boutique in Amsterdam, is known
for its quality denim selection.
Situated on Haarlemmerstraat since
2012, the shop has a solid range of
labels that is regularly updated.

"Every era can be described
in a signature pair of jeans that
underscores the relevance of this
timeless wardrobe item," says
co-founder Menno van Meurs.
Sitting on raw wooden shelves
in the industrial-style space are
brands such as Acne Studios and
Libertine Libertine, as well as the
shop's own collaborative products.
92–94 Haarlemmerstraat 92, 1013 EV
+31 (0)20 331 2778
tenuedenimes.com

②
Wildernis, Oud-West
Urban jungle

Terracotta pots, tiny cacti and
house plants are artfully arranged
around this lovely shop. A hub
for urbanites wanting a bit of
greenery for their homes, Wildernis
demonstrates what is possible
even in the smallest of spaces.

"There's a growing realisation
that our city is getting busier
and we have to take care of it
and make sure the environment
stays green for everyone," says
co-founder Mila van de Wall.
"People are also realising that
plants in the house are important
for their health."
165F Bilderdijkstraat, 1053 KP
+31 (0)20 785 2517
wildernisamsterdam.nl

③
Marie-Stella-Maris, Centrum
Thirsty work

Marie-Stella-Maris opened in 2014, inspired by a social incentive to support water projects around the world. The two-storey flagship immaculately displays a selection of room sprays, perfumes and natural skincare products. For each Marie-Stella-Maris item purchased, a fixed amount is donated to a clean drinking-water project.

Greenery, eye-catching typography and well-placed mirrors enliven the shopping experience and a passionate team is on hand to explain the brand's unique mission.
357HS Keizersgracht, 1016 EJ
+31 (0)85 273 2845
marie-stella-maris.com

Buy the whole bunch and maybe I'll let you buy me a generer too

Good for the soles
———
Famed trainer boutique Solebox is a mecca for sneakerheads but you'll easily mistake this outpost for a laboratory. The clinically clean environment creates the perfect backdrop for a selection of high-tops and low-cut trainers to suit all tastes.
solebox.com

⑥
Tommy Page, Centrum
History boy

From the best British tweed jackets
to durable knitwear, quality men's
vintage is sold at this well-stocked
establishment, which sits in the De
9 Straatjes shopping precinct.

Owner Tommy Page is typically
on hand to lend sartorial advice.
His opinion is one to be trusted
too, as the fashion designer turned
vintage purveyor is an expert on
the various cuts and styles of all
ages of fashion, from Victorian
rowing jackets to mod suits, all
of which are available here.
7 Prinsenstraat, 1015 DA
+31 (0)20 330 7941
tommypage.nl

Secondhand and vintage

01 **Salon Heleen Hülsmann,
Oud-Zuid:** You won't be
disappointed here. Find
secondhand high-end
designer gems from
recent collections.
salonheleenhulsmann.nl

02 **Second New Wardrobe,
Centrum:** Second New
Wardrobe offers barely
worn designer clothing,
as well as samples
straight off the runway.
324HS Kerkstraat, 1017 HC

03 **De Ruilhoek, De Pijp:**
De Ruilhoek's charm lies
in its friendly staff and
jam-packed space. You
really need to dig around
but if you don't mind
rolling up your sleeves you
might just end up with a
designer jewel for a steal.
deruilhoek.nl

④
Pompon, Jordaan
Bloomin' marvellous

In a city flowering with florists,
Pompon stands out as one of
Amsterdam's best and most
adventurous. The rich, intense
colours and arrangements often
bring to mind the paintings of
17th-century Dutch masters.

Co-owners Hilde Baart
(*pictured*) and husband Joost are
constantly searching for interesting
forms of floral expression and
specialise in hand-bound bouquets
of wildflowers. "After almost 30
years of running this business I still
get excited about a small, freshly
cut bunch of rare flowers," she says.
8-10 Prinsengracht, 1015 DV
+31 (0)20 622 5137
pomponshop.nl

⑤
Ace & Tate, Centrum
Clear vision

Puns aside, eyewear retailer Ace
& Tate is a visionary brand. Its
idea to cut the excess out of the
industry and deliver fashionable
yet affordable glasses has led to its
rapid success. What started as an
online-only service now has three
outposts across Amsterdam but the
attractive price point and quality
haven't changed.

The brand's sleek Centrum
outlet offers eye tests and one-
hour services for prescription-lens
fittings. The handsome frames are
displayed on shelves designed by
Dutch agency Occult Studios.
20 Huidenstraat, 1016 ES
+31 (0)20 261 8920
aceandtate.nl

Books and records
Type and tunes

②
Mendo, Centrum
Creative credentials

Co-founded by entrepreneur
Roy Rietstap and graphic designer
Joost Albronda, and designed
by Concrete Architectural
Associates, this inky interiored
shop stocks an impressive
collection of beautiful titles.

Pick up the finest books
on photography and fashion –
such as monographs of Henrik
Purienne, Mario Testino and Carli
Hermès – as well as those on the
art of interior and graphic design,
travel and cooking. Don't miss
Mendo's in-house imprint either.
11 Berenstraat, 1016 GG
+31 (0)20 612 1216
mendo.nl

①
Architectura & Natura, Centrum
Building boom

While pottering amid the canals,
cobbled streets and handsome
terraces of the city centre,
make sure to stop by bookshop
Architectura & Natura. Titles cover
varied subjects such as urbanism
and landscape gardening and are
available in Dutch and English.

The shop also publishes tomes
on architecture, from reference titles
on FA Warners who rose to fame
in the Amsterdam School to books
on urban renewal. There's plenty
here not just for the professional
architect but for those who have an
appreciation of the form.
22 Leliegracht, 1015 DG
+31 (0)20 623 6186
architectura.nl

Record shops

Synonymous with good music, Amsterdam is a magnet for vinyl collectors. The availability of both new and used records is dizzying.

01 Waxwell Records, Centrum: As well as selling records from hip-hop to reggae, this shop connects customers with collectors and can take old LPs off your hands. *waxwell.com*

02 Second Life Records, Jordaan: As its name suggests, this is where record fans can resurrect used vinyl and CDs from a cluttered collection of myriad genres. *secondlifemusic.nl*

03 Red Light Records, Centrum: Ring the buzzer and enter a bordello of good music, where funk, jazz, progressive, world, pop, rock, wave, disco and house albums circulate under moody lighting. *redlightrecordsamsterdam. com*

04 Vintage Voudou, Centrum: This is where Amsterdam's DJs come in search of tropical sounds that are becoming increasingly in vogue, from the Caribbean to Caracas. *vintagevoudou.com*

By the time this record's stopped spinning I'll have bought 45 more

③
Rush Hour Records, Centrum
On the record

Don't be fooled by the look and feel of this record shop. Rush Hour Records might appear to be all about electronic music but it stocks an extremely broad spectrum of genres, from mellow bossa nova to upbeat synth pop.

Founded in 1997, the label and shop have evolved into a sanctuary for music enthusiasts who come here from far and wide. Its selection of collectables and hard-to-find gems underscores why nothing beats browsing in person. The staff's involvement and passion is what sets the shop apart.
*116 Spuistraat, 1012 VA
+31 (0)20 427 4505
rushhour.nl*

④
Athenaeum Nieuwscentrum, Centrum
Best of print

Since this print treasure trove opened in 1969, its stock has continued to reflect its changing clientele. The strong Dutch graphic-design scene has brought about a growing number of independent magazines, which are proudly stocked here on heaving wooden shelves alongside everything from Belgian art titles to US weeklies. More than a shop, the Athenaeum brings people together and regularly hosts events and informal Q&A sessions with magazine editors and publishers.
*14-16 Spui, 1012 XA
+31 (0)20 514 1470
athenaeum.nl*

⑤
The American Book Center,
Centrum
Bibliophiles delight

Home to one of the largest
collections of English literature in
continental Europe, The American
Book Center started off as a small
bargain bookshop in 1972.

Today literary classics and
poetry sit side by side with manga,
science fiction and new-age titles.
Each section is curated by its own
buyer, who is "a matchmaker
between ideas and the readers",
according to co-owner Lynn
Kaplanian. The shop also features
an Espresso Book Machine that
allows on-demand book printing.
12 Spui, 1012 XA
+ 31 (0)20 625 5537
abc.nl

Vintage markets

01 Noordermarkt, Jordaan:
On Mondays you'll find
antiques, textiles and
records. On Saturdays
Noordermarkt sells organic
fruit, vegetables and
candles (*see page 41*).
noordermarkt-amsterdam.nl

02 IJ-Hallen, Noord: The
biggest flea market in
Europe takes place 15
times a year and offers
25 tennis courts' worth
of secondhand goods.
ijhallen.nl

03 Waterloopleinmarkt,
Centrum: Shoppers come
here for jewellery, bags,
bikes and other bits and
bobs. Someone once
picked up a painting by
artist Karel Appel for just
a couple of euros, so who
knows what you might find.
waterlooplein.amsterdam

Things we'd buy
—— Talking shops

Dutch design tends to teeter on the line between intrinsically practical and brazenly playful. Neon printed blankets and tea towels spun from the plushest of fabrics, teardrop-shaped hot-water bottles in fuzzy felt, a book the size of your palm and dainty ceramic coffee cups inspired by pleated paper: there are plenty of good-looking, intelligent products to take home.

Of course, you can't leave the Dutch capital without picking up one or two of the classics as well, from handsome bike accessories to fresh tulips, cumin-spiced cheese, *genever* and Dick Bruna's *Miffy* (or *Nijntje*, as she's known to the Dutch) books. Start shopping and fill your luggage with some of our top picks.

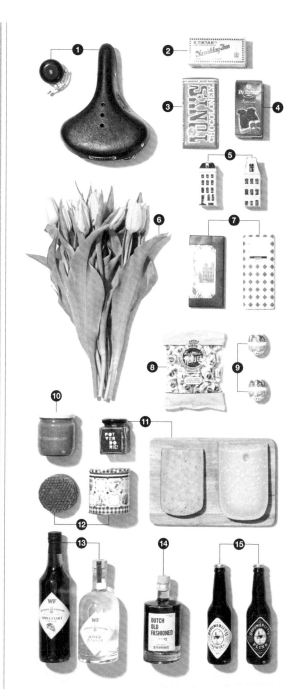

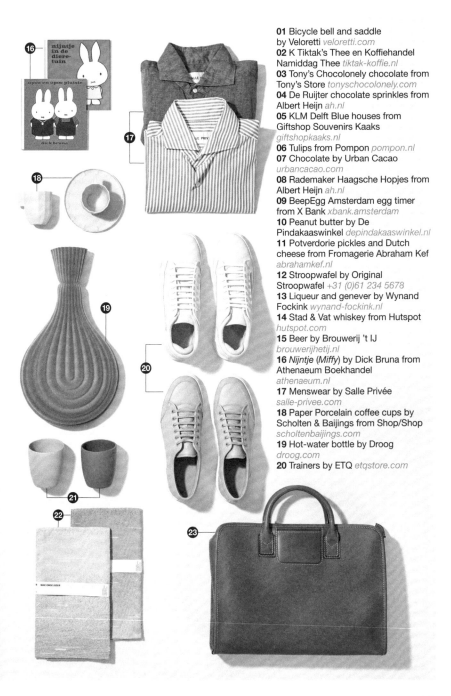

01 Bicycle bell and saddle by Veloretti *veloretti.com*
02 K Tiktak's Thee en Koffiehandel Namiddag Thee *tiktak-koffie.nl*
03 Tony's Chocolonely chocolate from Tony's Store *tonyschocolonely.com*
04 De Ruijter chocolate sprinkles from Albert Heijn *ah.nl*
05 KLM Delft Blue houses from Giftshop Souvenirs Kaaks *giftshopkaaks.nl*
06 Tulips from Pompon *pompon.nl*
07 Chocolate by Urban Cacao *urbancacao.com*
08 Rademaker Haagsche Hopjes from Albert Heijn *ah.nl*
09 BeepEgg Amsterdam egg timer from X Bank *xbank.amsterdam*
10 Peanut butter by De Pindakaaswinkel *depindakaaswinkel.nl*
11 Potverdorie pickles and Dutch cheese from Fromagerie Abraham Kef *abrahamkef.nl*
12 Stroopwafel by Original Stroopwafel *+31 (0)61 234 5678*
13 Liqueur and genever by Wynand Fockink *wynand-fockink.nl*
14 Stad & Vat whiskey from Hutspot *hutspot.com*
15 Beer by Brouwerij 't IJ *brouwerijhetij.nl*
16 *Nijntje (Miffy)* by Dick Bruna from Athenaeum Boekhandel *athenaeum.nl*
17 Menswear by Salle Privée *salle-privee.com*
18 Paper Porcelain coffee cups by Scholten & Baijings from Shop/Shop *scholtenbaijings.com*
19 Hot-water bottle by Droog *droog.com*
20 Trainers by ETQ *etqstore.com*

21 Bone porcelain cups from Hutspot *hutspot.com*
22 Mae Engelgeer tea towels from Restored *restored.nl*
23 Leather briefcase by Travelteq *travelteq.com*
24 Glasses by Ace & Tate *aceandtate.nl*
25 The Cool Club playing cards from Hutspot *hutspot.com*

26 Irma Boom-designed museum guide from Rijksmuseum *rijksmuseum.nl*
27 *Irma Boom: The Architecture of the Book* from Athenaeum Boekhandel *athenaeum.nl*
28 Vintage scarf from Tommy Page *tommypage.nl*
29 Vintage film poster from Eye Filmmuseum *eyefilm.nl*

30 Taiko's Gin by Conservatorium Hotel *conservatoriumhotel.com*
31 *Bedankt Sorry Hoera!* Dutch phrase book from Sissy-Boy *sissy-boy.com*
32 Jeans from Tenue de Nîmes *tenuedenimes.com*
33 Scholten & Baijings Colour Plaid blanket from Shop/Shop *scholtenbaijings.com*

12 essays
— All about Amsterdam

Mind your head
Walking with giants
by Pauline den Hartog Jager,
journalist

Movie nights
Sophisticated cinema
by Brian Maston,
film festival co-director

Wheels of fortune
Cycling in the city
by Joleen Goffin,
Monocle

Dutch masters
We need your help
by Hans den Hartog Jager,
art critic

Finding 'gezellig'
A feel for the city
by Venetia Rainey,
Monocle

Life goals
Lesson in football
by Dan Poole,
writer

'Dam creative
The city's design scene
by Carole Baijings,
designer

Land, liberals and Lennon
History in a nutshell
by Mikaela Aitken,
writer

From silk to silicon
Next-generation start-ups
by Yoko Choy,
journalist

What's your type?
Every letter tells a story
by Ramiro Espinoza,
type designer

After dark
The night manager
by Mirik Milan,
former night mayor

Full circle
Dutch food gets a makeover
by Vicky Hampton,
food writer

What better way to discover the city than by hammock?

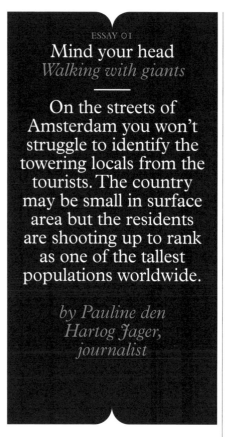

ESSAY 01

Mind your head
Walking with giants

On the streets of Amsterdam you won't struggle to identify the towering locals from the tourists. The country may be small in surface area but the residents are shooting up to rank as one of the tallest populations worldwide.

by Pauline den Hartog Jager, journalist

More than half of the Netherlands lies below sea level and, besides building better dykes to protect the country from the encroaching water, we Dutch have found a natural way to survive global warming: by making sure our heads are above water.

It's no secret that the Dutch are a lanky lot. With an average height of 1.83 metres, Dutch men are the world's tallest, while Dutch women (1.7 metres) are second only to their Latvian counterparts. If you're still not convinced, the Club for Tall People in the Netherlands requires its female members to be taller than 1.8 metres and male members taller than 1.9 metres. There are about 900,000 people in the Netherlands taller than 1.9 metres and an astounding 60,000 of them are more than 2 metres tall.

Visitors to the Dutch capital can experience subtle knock-on effects from walking among giants. Bathroom mirrors and showerheads are almost unreachable and attending a concert can offer little more of a view than the shoulders in front of you. But don't worry, you're not alone.

I'm 1.78 metres tall and am by far the shortest in my family. My younger sisters are 1.83 metres and 1.87 metres, with my parents somewhere in between. To greet my cousins with the customary three kisses, I have to strain to reach their towering frames (1.97 metres and 2.05 metres respectively). It wasn't until I moved to the UK that I realised I'm not that short at all by non-Dutch standards. I often get asked to grab something from the top shelf in the supermarket and standing in a packed Tube is far less claustrophobic when you are able to catch some air.

Still, I have no reason to complain about my height: I fit most regular-sized clothes, my shoe size is about average, I can ride a bike with a regular frame and I won't hit my head when entering a house. Many Dutch citizens, however, face height-related challenges on a daily basis. Where to buy shirts that aren't crop tops? How to find a zippy city car with enough legroom? The real issues start when we travel abroad: urinals are too low, showerheads neglect anything above chest height and beds are too short. It can also be a painful experience: I once ended up with concussion after smashing my head against a ceiling beam.

High and mighty
———
01 **Tijs Verwest, 1.88 metres**
Famous DJ, known as
DJ Tiësto.
02 **Famke Janssen,
1.82 metres**
Actress and former Bond girl
in *Goldeneye*.
03 **Rob Bruintjes, 2.21 metres**
Chairman of the Dutch
Foundation for Tall
People.

"Bathroom mirrors are almost unreachable and attending a concert can offer little more of a view than the shoulders in front of you"

Luckily for its giants, the Netherlands has solutions: bikes come in different frame sizes, more fashion brands produce longer jeans and higher kitchen tabletops are becoming the homeware shop default. There are also support groups, organisations, and magazines dedicated to the extremely tall. Among them, Stichting Lange Mensen (Foundation for Tall People) and Klub Lange Mensen (Club for Tall People) help support the rights of the Dutch giants, including their ongoing battle for more legroom on airplanes.

The Netherlands also ranks as one of the nations that produces the most top models but you won't spot many locals wearing killer heels; trainers are perfectly acceptable in most bars and pubs. Even the policymakers are helping out: in 2003 the minimum ceiling height for new-build houses was increased from 2.4 to 2.6 metres.

The Dutch haven't always been so lofty. The average male height today is 20cm higher than 150 years ago. But the cause of our long limbs is contentious. Is it genetics, fresh air or healthcare? Are we really evolving in reaction to those rising tides or is it simply our affinity with cheese and milk?

According to recent studies the answer is more obvious: genetics. Tall people tend to marry other tall people and tall men tend to have more children than their shorter countrymen. The curve hasn't slowed, which means plenty more opportunities for inventive solutions to cater to an ever-growing population. In height, that is. — (M)

ABOUT THE WRITER: Pauline den Hartog Jager is a London-based film-maker and journalist and was previously MONOCLE's video journalist. Whenever she returns to the Netherlands she picks up a block (or two) of Old Amsterdam cheese.

ESSAY 02
Movie nights
Sophisticated cinema
———

Going to the pictures in Amsterdam doesn't have to mean spending time in a modern multiplex. For added nostalgia, follow the locals to an art deco gem – you might even catch a homegrown film.

*by Brian Maston,
film festival co-director*

On a sunny day in Los Angeles in 1994, a ponytailed John Travolta describes to Samuel L Jackson the particular joys of going to the cinema in the Dutch capital. "You can walk into a movie theatre in Amsterdam and buy a beer. And I don't mean just, like, no paper cup – I'm talking about a *glass* of beer."

This scene introduces hitmen Jules and Vincent in Quentin Tarantino's neo-noir classic *Pulp Fiction*. Tarantino wrote the script for the film while holed up in the Dutch capital. He immediately recognised the cinema culture in the city as something quite unique when compared with the suburban multiplexes of the time.

In that regard, little about the movie-going experience has changed in Amsterdam since the 1990s – or the 1920s for that matter. While the city has several modern cinemas, its chic, well-heeled youth still tends to prefer the traditional movie houses built in the early 20th century to today's soulless big-box cinemas. Gothic and elegant Tuschinski receives the most attention and is often the site of major Dutch film premieres but cosy neighbourhood cinema The Movies offers an authentic and lively cinematic experience. Housed in a narrow and unassuming shopfront, the venue opens up to reveal four screens and a spacious art deco café and restaurant, along with a candlelit wooden bar. Going to the cinema is a social occasion in Amsterdam and, while informal, no one shows up in a tracksuit. And yes, you can take your beer into the theatre.

Amsterdam's cinemas show a variety of independent and international films, which can make it hard for native-born film-makers to compete. The Dutch film industry has yet to produce a unique international style such as Italian neorealismo or French nouvelle vague. Popular Dutch films tend to mostly reproduce Hollywood genres such as romcoms and action films. At the other end of the spectrum are the festival films that don't reach much of an audience at all beyond critics and film buffs.

"Going to the cinema is a social occasion in Amsterdam and, while informal, no one shows up in a tracksuit"

But it's no real blow to national pride to point this out: the Dutch are well aware of their film industry's shortcomings. For many years, Dutch films were synonymous with poor acting and gratuitous sex scenes. Since the 1970s, sex has been Dutch film-makers' go-to method for attracting audiences and creating a buzz around their work. One of the more proficient purveyors of this aesthetic is that looming giant of the Dutch film industry, Paul Verhoeven. Sex and sexuality have been recurring themes in his films, from the lauded 1977 Second World War classic *Soldier of Orange* to Golden Globe-winning *Elle*, which was released in 2016.

Verhoeven is one of the few Dutch directors to have "made it big" in Hollywood but, over the years, he's had his share of critics on both sides of the Atlantic. He was more or less exiled to Hollywood in the early 1980s after making some controversial films and in some circles is still remembered for making the worst film of the 1990s: *Showgirls*. But after having built up a career in LA directing blockbusters such as *RoboCop*, *Total Recall* and *Basic Instinct*, he was welcomed home again with open arms.

To a Dutch audience, Verhoeven will most likely be remembered for *Turkish Delight*, a generation-defining film made in 1973 that has contributed to the collective visual consciousness of the Netherlands. The film portrays the tumultuous affair of a young artistic couple, Eric and Olga. It documents their love life in a natural fashion that may be too raw for current audiences accustomed to a more photoshopped version of human intimacy.

Eric and Olga love, fight, kick and scream their way through polite bourgeois society, eventually exhausting each other and the viewer but not before providing one of the most inspiring moments of Dutch cinema: the two of them riding together on one bicycle, laughing and weaving their way through Amsterdam traffic after getting married. The relationship, inevitably, does not last but this iconic image of the two young lovers has survived.

While Verhoeven continues to be relevant even in the twilight of his career, a new generation of Dutch film-makers have stepped up and assumed the reins. They are making films that are both cosmopolitan and local. A good example is Jim Taihuttu's gangster flick *Wolf*, which details the life of a Dutch-Moroccan kickboxer amid the grey landscape of urban Dutch society. The film charts the rise and fall of an immigrant antihero who climbs the socioeconomic ladder like Tony Montana in *Scarface* and punches his way through life like Jake LaMotta in *Raging Bull*. Adaptations from Dutch literature also remain popular, such as the introspective *Tonio*, about love and family tragedy in the Amsterdam literary scene.

Dutch films are becoming more sophisticated and polished, with the old clichés about convenient sex scenes and wooden dialogue slowly disappearing. The country now produces film-makers, documentarians and animators who will some day dominate the silver screens of Amsterdam's sleek cinemas. — (M)

Top cinemas in Amsterdam
———
01 The Movies
Authentic cinema with a lively bar and restaurant scene.
02 Pathé Tuschinski
Classic movie palace in the heart of the city.
03 FilmHallen
Neighbourhood cinema with tasty street food.

ABOUT THE WRITER: Brian Maston is co-director of CampusDoc Film Festival and a senior lecturer in film and media. He's also a proud resident of Amsterdam, a film buff and someone who is willing to give Verhoeven's *RoboCop* a second chance.

ESSAY 03
Wheels of fortune
Cycling in the city
———
What's the first thing you do when you arrive in Amsterdam? Get yourself a granny bike, adopt the upright position of a member of the royal family and take control of the road.

by Joleen Goffin,
Monocle

Call me naïve but as a Flemish-speaking Belgian I thought it was safe to assume that the Dutch and I would have plenty in common. Beyond a border, history and language, it's true that we also share a love of bicycles. From a young age we pedal our way to independence: I was six when I made my first solo journey to school. However, the first time I travelled to Amsterdam to visit a friend, it soon became clear that when it comes to cycling, the Dutch do things differently.

As I confidently mounted my bike at Centraal station, I wasn't prepared for what lay ahead. Almost immediately I was manoeuvred to the side by an overtaking cyclist. I was struck not only by the bravado of the Dutch cyclists but also that of my usually demure friend. With a bluster I had never witnessed she cleared herself a path with voice and bell (I know that's the purpose of a bell but in Belgium it's considered impolite to use it). And as we whisked past unsuspecting tourists, I

caught glimpses of their flabbergasted faces. Ten minutes later we arrived. No dawdling – this was serious work.

It's taken a few trips but I think I've finally cracked cycling in the city. It's a thrilling experience to be part of a swarm of starlings moving as if choreographed, crossing busy junctions, navigating our way through the city, weaving between cars and pedestrians. It may seem like chaos to the onlooker but to the participants it's highly organised.

Perhaps the key to success is the Dutch granny bike. It may weigh a tonne but its design ensures that your posture is regimental-straight which, in turn, inspires a new level of confidence: you feel like a royal on a horse. And if you're the queen you don't need a helmet: everyone else will look out for you. It sounds strange but Dutch drivers likely grew up on a bike so they anticipate your behaviour. It's a stark contrast to the slinky Lycra pelotons in cities such as London and New York, always attempting to extract respect from motorists. In Amsterdam it's that posture that makes you feel as if you own the road.

Or maybe it's the fact that Dutch cyclists don't follow the rules: the rules follow them. I still make mistakes and it's terrifying. On one occasion, while reporting for this guide, I was the first in a queue of bikes waiting at a red light. When I realised I was about to pedal in the wrong direction, I froze. My explanation was lost in the flurry of commuters and I received a grating concerto of bicycle bells and colourful phrases – some of which I didn't even know existed in our language.

This anarchy didn't happen overnight: cycling in the Netherlands has a history. Troops of cyclists would slow down

"It's a thrilling experience to be part of a swarm of starlings moving as if choreographed, navigating our way through the city"

Pedal to the metal
—
01 881,000
Number of bicycles
in the city.
02 15,000
Number of bikes that end
up in the canals each year.
03 2,000,000km
Combined distance
cycled by Amsterdammers
every day.

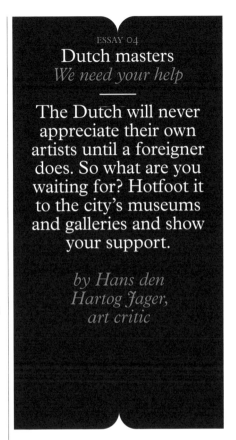

ESSAY 04
Dutch masters
We need your help
—

The Dutch will never appreciate their own artists until a foreigner does. So what are you waiting for? Hotfoot it to the city's museums and galleries and show your support.

by Hans den Hartog Jager, art critic

German occupiers during the Second World War by riding in the middle of the road but the critical change happened in the 1970s when the government made huge investment in infrastructure. For almost every Belgian this made the Netherlands a place of pilgrimage to visit on a cycling holiday. As a kid I remember knowing the exact moment we crossed the border: when the bumpy road beneath our wheels turned to pristine asphalt.

Some argue that Amsterdam has become a victim of its own success. Bikes now outnumber people and, if this two-wheeled transport is not your thing, you might consider it, as my colleague coined it bluntly, "bike pollution".

But schemes for more underground (and underwater) bike parking are being developed. And all of this feels like a nice problem to have if you compare it to capitals where the car is still king. The health and environmental benefits of cycling are many but beyond that, there are few better ways to explore the city. So when you visit Amsterdam, do as the locals do and find yourself a granny bike. Sit up straight, act confident and don't be intimidated. You'll soon feel the thrill and blend into the rush of starlings – just don't freeze at the lights. — (M)

ABOUT THE WRITER: Joleen Goffin can usually be found producing radio shows for Monocle 24. But as a native Dutch speaker she couldn't wait to hop off her office chair and into the saddle to whiz around Amsterdam's best culture, design and architecture hotspots.

Us Dutch have always had a complicated relationship with our artistic past. We are a very small nation, founded on extremely flat land that for centuries has been threatened by water. The country has also been flooded with something else: Calvinism. These factors have all left distinctive traces and it's surely no accident that one of the most quoted expressions to summarise the Dutch national character is: "Act normal, that's already strange enough." And then we, as a people, so proud of our normality, produced artists such as Rembrandt (dark and bankrupt), Johannes Vermeer (shy and bankrupt), Frans Hals (almost bankrupt and couldn't draw a straight line) and, well, Van Gogh. Yes, Van Gogh was Dutch.

So it should come as no surprise that it took a fair amount of rumbling and groaning before the Dutch acknowledged the power of our best artists – Rembrandt, the national Calvinistic treasure, being the only exception. At the beginning of the 19th century, after the Netherlands had been ruled by the French for decades, artists such as Hals and Vermeer were collectively all but forgotten. It took a French art critic, Théophile Thoré-Bürger, to point the Dutch back in the direction of their own artistic heritage. Not only did Thoré-Bürger write about artists such as Hals, Vermeer and Fabritius, he also put his money where his mouth was and bought their paintings, including Fabritius's now-famous "Goldfinch" (1654). This was an effective way of

"Please, non-Dutch reader, continue to help us. Give us the recognition we need so we can keep appreciating our own artists"

Alternative bests

01 Rembrandt
"Syndics of the Drapers' Guild" (better than "The Night Watch")
02 Johannes Vermeer
"The Milkmaid" (better than "Girl with a Pearl Earring")
03 Frans Hals
"Portrait of a Couple" (better than "The Merry Drinker")

persuading the Dutch of his sincerity: the Netherlands, after all, has always been a nation of trade.

Since then this attitude towards Dutch artists has prevailed: everything is poppycock until foreigners say the opposite. The best illustration of this is the story of Paulus Potter's "The Bull" (1647). In the late-18th century this was a moderately appreciated painting until the French invaded, looted some Dutch artwork and carried them to France. "The Bull" was displayed in a prominent spot in the Louvre and everyone fell for the realistic bravado of the painting. After 20 years in France it became a beloved classic – and, of course, that caught the attention of the Dutch. So when Napoleon was defeated, one of the first things the Dutch did was bring "The Bull" home. It was carried to The Hague as part of a large parade, accompanied by military honours and church bells. Only then was a classic born.

Gaining foreign recognition has become standard procedure for a Dutch artist to attract domestic appreciation. Traditionally, most artists of merit don't wait for this and move abroad instead: Van Gogh went to France; Mondrian to France and then the US. In fact, almost every Dutch artist to have become famous has lived abroad, including Willem de Kooning, Karel Appel, Armando, Constant Nieuwenhuys, Bas Jan Ader, Ger van Elk, Daan van Golden, Michael Raedecker and Mark Manders. And the ones who stay tend only to be taken seriously after their first international shows; think of Marlene Dumas (Moma, Tate), Rineke Dijkstra (SF Moma, Guggenheim) and Aernout Mik (Moma). But after that the reward is great and everyone in the Netherlands applauds your success.

So please, dear non-Dutch reader, continue to help us. Give us the recognition we need so we can keep appreciating our own artists. Go to the Rijksmuseum to see Rembrandt, Vermeer, Hals, Fabritius, Dou and Verspronck. Queue in that bloody long line for Van Gogh, one of our national treasures (the line I mean, not the museum). By doing so you help us compensate for our small-country insecurities – and the artwork in the museum is supposed to be great. Or so we are told. — (M)

ABOUT THE WRITER: Hans den Hartog Jager is a writer and art critic based in Amsterdam. He writes for *NRC Handelsblad*, *Artforum International* and various other magazines. He has published more than 10 books, mainly about contemporary art.

ESSAY 05
Finding 'gezellig'
A feel for the city
———

Whether you're out with friends or travelling alone, find yourself a comfy chair in a *bruin* café, order some snacks and chill out. Dutch-style.

by Venetia Rainey, Monocle

If there's a word that sums up the best of Dutch culture it's *gezellig*. The under-appreciated sibling of the Danish concept *hygge*, *gezellig* is one of those tangly words whose meaning unravels through experience rather than a neat dictionary definition.

Gezellig is an afternoon of games with the family. It's a natter over coffee with an old friend, or laying side by side with your partner in bed reading a book after a long day. It's the neighbour who always stops to say hi or that unpretentious pub where the staff know you by name. It's a plate of deep-fried snacks to share or a cat curling up on your lap when you're ill. Cosy, I think you'll agree, doesn't cover it.

Gezellig, or *gezelligheid* to use the noun, doesn't put on airs and doesn't photograph well. It's less concerned with how things look than how they feel and, as such, it will probably never become as fashionable as its Danish counterpart. The Dutch don't mind though: they're too busy enjoying the good things in life to worry about it.

But for any visitor to the Netherlands, understanding *gezelligheid* is crucial and getting yourself into a *hartstikke gezellige* (really *gezellig*) situation should be top of the bucket list. So how to go about it?

> *"The spirit of 'gezellig' is good company, that reaffirming feeling of being in the presence of others, whether you know them or not"*

A good place to start is with a *borrel*, an informal evening gathering with friends (old or new), preferably at an old-school *bruin* café (brown café) such as Café Welling (*see page 45*). Brown cafés, so-called because of the walls and ceilings stained from decades of pre-ban smoking, are temples to the *gezelligheid* doctrine.

Forget about trendy craft beer and fusion bar snacks. These are places for several *fluitjes* (small glasses) of the local pilsner and some traditional Dutch finger food known as *borrelhapjes*. *Bitterballen* – a deep-fried, golden ball of gooey roux flecked with meat (*see page 41*) – is the king of the *borrelhapjes* but other great contestants include *ossenworst* (raw beef sausage), cubes of old Dutch cheese with some sharp mustard, or a boiled egg.

Travelling solo? Not to worry. Grab a newspaper (or this book) and stake out a corner table at your *bruin* café of choice, being sure to position your chair so you're facing into the room. It's important that you're not closed off from everyone else, even if you don't plan on chatting.

That's because *gezelligheid* isn't all about food and drink. No, the spirit of *gezellig* is good company, that reaffirming feeling of being in the presence of others, whether you know them or not. The word is actually derived from *gezel*, an old term for a companion or fellow that contains the Germanic root *sal*: a place where people gather. The word's meaning has expanded over the past millennium but at its heart *gezellig* still describes a scenario where people take pleasure from being around each other (or even a pet).

Which brings me to *gezellig's* evil twin: *ongezellig*. This should be avoided. It means coming home to a cold, empty house after work and eating alone, or being made to feel unwelcome among friends. Someone using their phone throughout a meal is supremely *ongezellig*, as is a restaurant with unfriendly staff.

While the Dutch can't control the sort of people you hang out with, they are masters at creating the right sort of environment in their restaurants, cafés and bars. Low lighting, comfortable chairs and a warm atmosphere: these are crucial elements of the Dutch hospitality industry (there's a reason Amsterdam is such a joy to wine and dine your way around). All of the food and drink suggestions in this guidebook ooze *gezelligheid* – except for, perhaps, the herring stall, and even that could be *gezellig* if visited on a sunny day.

The only thing left to explain about *gezellig* is how to pronounce it. It's ge-*zell*-ig, and the first and last "g" should come from the back of the throat. If that's too tricky, never mind: it's not as important as actually experiencing it. And the Dutch will always find it *gezellig* that you tried. — (M)

ABOUT THE WRITER: Venetia Rainey is MONOCLE's Business editor. She is also half Dutch and thus constantly in search of *gezelligheid*.

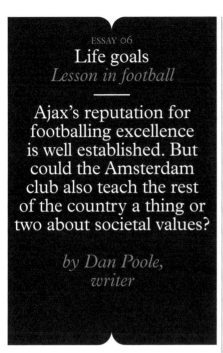

ESSAY 06
Life goals
Lesson in football

———

Ajax's reputation for footballing excellence is well established. But could the Amsterdam club also teach the rest of the country a thing or two about societal values?

by Dan Poole, writer

Granted, it's not often that the words "football team" and "laudable social model" crop up in the same sentence – but they just have so hold on to your hats. Or rather, for the benefit of a drawn-out metaphor, hold on to your crotch. That way I can be the free-kick taker, this essay can be the ball, you can be part of the wall and the goal can be me convincing you that not everything to do with this sport is rotten and fetid.

My instrument of persuasion is Ajax (pronounced "aye-ax") Amsterdam, the Netherlands' most famous club. Its mythical status – it's named after a Greek hero, no less – was sealed at the beginning of the 1970s when it

won three European Cups in a row (which doesn't happen very often). The conductor of this footballing symphony was Dutch player Johan Cruyff, who was so talented that he had a move named after him (the Cruyff turn) and is credited with having changed the way that the game is played worldwide.

And here's the thing: such is the manner in which Ajax is run that there are lessons to be learned for the rest of the country. And we're not talking about perfecting a one-touch pass or how to head a ball without falling over; this is about an ethos and vision that applies as much off the pitch as it does on it.

"How did this ideology come about, this commitment to not only think of the children but look after employees from top to bottom?"

But first let's take a look at an area in which Ajax excels but that the rest of the country needs no help with whatsoever: the recognition that the children are our future. Ajax's world-renowned youth system was set up from the club's inception in 1900 and has been churning out exceptionally talented players ever since – most Dutch and many from Amsterdam or the surrounding area. For example, when the team won the European Cup for a fourth time in 1995, eight members of the starting line-up were graduates of the club's academy.

But the Netherlands also scores well in this department. A 2013 Unicef survey established that Dutch children are the happiest in the world, based on metrics including education, health and environment. The country also wins out when it comes to youth unemployment, with two thirds of under-25s in jobs compared with less than half across all OECD-member countries.

So, well played everyone. But it's at the other end of the spectrum that the rest of the country lags behind. A 2016 survey into Dutch people's attitudes towards their older relatives found that two thirds believe it is the government's remit to look after the elderly; indeed, said government is among the top tax spenders in Europe when it comes to senior care. And while Geert Wilders' early-2017 efforts to oust Mark Rutte as PM were divisive at best, one of his claims that most people supported was that the country's elderly are neglected, with risible conditions in many care homes.

Ajax, however, takes a very different approach to its retirees. Now, admittedly we're not talking about OAPs here but the relative brevity of a career in this sport means that footballer years are a bit like dog years. And for most players who have panted their last

breath on the pitch, the best they can expect from their parent club is a nebulous ambassadorial role. But Ajax? It gainfully re-employs its elder statesmen.

In recent years Ronald de Boer, his twin brother Frank, Dennis Bergkamp, Jaap Stam and Marc Overmars have all returned to the club where they first made their names. And they've done so having plied their trade abroad – a classic example of a country's talent learning new skills on foreign shores before returning to the motherland to share newfound knowledge. And it's not just in a coaching capacity that they have been deployed; Overmars for example, once a wing wizard, is now technical director.

Then there's Edwin van der Sar. The former goalkeeper was at Ajax for nine years (which included that European Cup win in 1995) before going on to play for Juventus in Italy, then Fulham and Manchester United in England. But once he'd hung up his boots he did a master's in sports and brand management (at the Johan Cruyff Institute in Barcelona, naturally) and then got snapped up by Ajax as its marketing director in 2012.

"I was fortunate enough to return to this club as I owe all of my career to them," he said in 2014. "Now, I have a chance to give it back to the club where it all started. All the former players that are working here with me wanted to contribute at the club that helped us grow as players." The former shot-stopper could clearly walk the walk as well as talk the talk: he was promoted to CEO in 2016.

And how did this ideology come about, this commitment to not only think of the children but look after employees from top to bottom? That man Cruyff again. In 2010 he angrily proclaimed: "This isn't Ajax anymore." Orthodoxy duly challenged, that fabled youth system was refreshed and Van der Sar and friends, former players schooled in the Ajax way, were brought into the fold to inspire the next generation.

So if a system isn't working and a hierarchy has lost its way, the potential for change can be realised? There might well be a lesson for us all there. — (M)

Other things called Ajax
——
01 **Swedish singer**
Lisa Ajax has a song called "I Don't Give A". Cheeky.
02 **Racehorse**
Won the Grand Prix de Paris in 1904. Magnifique.
03 **Cleaning products**
Pronounced "Ay-jax". Confusing.

ABOUT THE WRITER: Dan Poole is MONOCLE's former chief sub editor and, when not tackling spelling mistakes or giving misplaced commas the red card, likes to watch his beloved Manchester United playing The Beautiful Game (he insisted on those capital letters).

ESSAY 07
'Dam creative
The city's design scene
——
Amsterdam's natural beauty and artistic heritage make it appealing to visit. And for designers who live and work here it's a constant source of inspiration and community.

by Carole Baijings, designer

Art and design are inextricably woven into daily life in Amsterdam; we're surrounded by museums housing the works of the most famous Dutch designers and artists. These venues have been part of the city's identity for a long time but other displays of art and design are everywhere, in the form of sculptures, benches, streetlights and great architecture. All of these different aspects fit together and present us with inspiring silhouettes.

Because the Netherlands is so flat it's almost as if the landscape has an ingrained sense of minimalism and I think that is in our DNA. There is a lot of colour around and maybe you see it more because everything is so flat. You see the play of

Floristry in the city
—
01 Pompon
Wild blooms at their best.
pompon.nl
02 Menno Kroon
Snap up some
elaborate bouquets.
mennokroon.nl
03 MC Bloom
Best for potted plants.
mcbloom.nl

light with the rising sun and again as it sets, as well as all of the different shades throughout the day, particularly across the canals and IJ harbour. Some of our most revered artists, including Mondrian, Van Gogh, Rietveld and Rembrandt, pioneered the way that the Dutch bring colour into art. All of this culminates to influence the way we work and design here. From the paintings in our galleries to the urban-planning of our neighbourhoods, design in the city is all about light, colour and the contrast between matte and gloss.

Another positive impact of our landscape is its size. The Netherlands is very small so it's easy, even though we're in a capital city, to connect and work closely with the craftsmen who make our prototypes. If you need something or someone, from a textile weaver to a skilled woodworker, you only have to drive for an hour – or three at most – to find it. This combination of the creativity fostered in the city and the skills that exist across the country has created a dynamic design scene in Amsterdam that is hard to come by in other cities. If you live in the centre of London it's much harder to find someone who has a welding factory who can make you a nice frame, or a carpenter you need for a piece of a furniture.

The art and design in our city helps to improve the quality of life and bring together the community. Summer sees the arrival of Art Zuid, when a 2.5km stretch of road is temporarily adorned with sculptures made by international artists;

Schiphol Airport is really close so staying connected with the global design scene is easy. The city also hosts free concerts on the canals, which fill with people in boats, and a hush descends as the floating crowd listens to the orchestra. Then in winter there is the Light Festival, which decorates Vondelpark and the canals with glittering and glowing sculptures.

A good example of what our design heritage means to the people is the area between the Rijksmuseum and the Stedelijk Museum. This space was occupied by a road that ran under the Rijksmuseum; during the renovations to the museum the architects considered closing the passage but Amsterdammers lobbied to keep it open. Today the tunnel is a thoroughfare for cyclists and the space between the museums is a beautiful square full of sporting activities and new buildings, including a supermarket with a green terraced roof for people to enjoy the sun.

Looking forward, the new generation is more focused on materials rather than form and the ones who are really finding their own way are doing things such as making their own machines to produce their own fabrics. They're also recycling a lot of materials and I think that's great. A good example are the glass bricks used by MVRDV in the Hooftstraat Chanel shop; they are very special.

So the city will continue to influence its creatives and in turn the new generation of creatives will influence the city. As a designer, it's a great place to live. — (M)

ABOUT THE WRITER: Carole Baijings is one of the most celebrated product designers in the Netherlands. Her young son Rem is already showing signs of becoming one of Amsterdam's designers of the future.

ESSAY 08

Land, liberals and Lennon
History in a nutshell

———

Founded on commerce that benefitted from dealing with all who docked, Amsterdam's liberal beginnings are still very much part of the city's fabric.

by Mikaela Aitken, writer

Some history books would have you believe that Amsterdam was founded by adventurers in hollowed-out logs but most Amsterdammers favour the fable of two fishermen and their dog. The trio were supposedly out on the North Sea when a storm rolled in, so they sought shelter along a stretch of river. Pulling up to land, the woozy hound tumbled from the boat and threw up, thus christening the land for Amsterdam. The factual accuracy of this may be dubious but old versions of the city's crest picture two men and a dog.

In the 12th century, fishermen and farmers encroached the peat swamps surrounding the Amstel river and forged dams and dykes to create low-lying land. One particularly hefty dam across the Amstel is rumoured to have given rise to the name Amsterdam. You can still visit it today although it looks a little different: its modern formation is Dam Square and the main drag, Damrak, sits where the river once ran. From here a medieval merchant

town expanded and was granted its first charter in 1300.

Trade of predominantly boats, beer and soused herring fuelled the economy but what really put the city on the map was, once again, vomit. In 1345 a dying man received his final Holy Communion, only to regurgitate the wafer whole. This holy mess was thrown on the fire but the wafer refused to burn. Heralded in likeness to its metaphorical representation of the body of Christ, Catholics declared it a miracle, a church was built on the site and European pilgrims flocked in.

Catholicism grew but the city's leaders practised tolerance, in part owing to open trade and the benefits of business dealings with anyone who docked, regardless of race or religion. Over the coming decades, Spain and the Catholic church tightened their hold on the Netherlands. At this time a young German-born nobleman, Willem of Nassau (or the Prince of Orange), was rising through the ranks of the Spanish court. After seeing the atrocities dealt to Protestants and non-Catholic believers at Spanish hands, he led a revolt and thus began the 80 Years' War, which lasted from 1566 to 1648. In 1584, Willem was murdered in Delft by a devout Catholic but his fight for liberalism inspired a nation and he was memorialised as the father of the Dutch Republic.

Despite the conflict, trade in Amsterdam proliferated. In 1599 the second Dutch expedition to Indonesia returned with a handsome bounty and this new era of commerce sparked the city's Golden Age. Wealth flowed in and the population grew. A new network of canals was added in a ring around the city centre and rows of houses were erected in the 17th century. In one such canal house, Dirck van Os welcomed anyone – Dutch or foreign – wishing to be a shareholder in the Dutch East India Company; this moment was arguably the inception of capitalism. The world's first stock exchange opened in 1602 and in 1655 city hall (now the Royal Palace) was built to

tower above the surrounding churches:
a sly reminder to the city's clergymen of
their inferior role.

Reliance on trade dampened with the
industrial revolution in the 19th century,
altering the topography of the city. The
western entrance to the IJ river was added
along with neighbourhoods, including
Westerpark and the Eastern Docklands.
Leading characters of this era were the
coquettish madams of the red-light
district. Continuing their historical
tolerance, lawmakers turned a blind eye to
prostitution (it was only legalised in 2000).

Twentieth-century protagonists
continued to guide the narrative of the
city, including the architects of the
Amsterdam School movement between
1910 and 1930 and banker Walraven van
Hall, who led a resistance against Nazi
occupation. It was also no accident
that John Lennon and Yoko Ono chose
Amsterdam as the stage for one of their
1969 bed-ins for peace. They were drawn
to the progressive capital, its vibrant
population and counterculture movement.
Fast-forward to the modern day and these
qualities still feel very much part of the
city's fabric. Vomit, fable, odd characters
and all, Amsterdam continues to uphold
its liberal disposition. — (M)

City of firsts
—
01 Modern family
The 17th-century canal house
was arguably the first take on
a modern family home.
02 Pump it up
The first pump-driven fire hose
appeared in 1672.
03 Love it
First capital to legalise gay
marriage (2001).

ABOUT THE WRITER: As editor of this guide, Mikaela
Aitken was raring to explore but she was kind of a
wimp when it came to cycling. Instead, she stuck to
navigating the canals, cathedrals and queasy tourists
on foot – a sensible move, she insists.

ESSAY 09
From silk to silicon
Next-generation start-ups
—
The brightest technology entrepreneurs are popping up where you would least expect them; Amsterdam is suddenly giving Silicon Valley a run for its money.
*by Yoko Choy,
journalist*

Think start-ups and, after Silicon Valley
pops into your head, aggressively emerging
economies (such as India or China) and
traditional major players on the world stage
(such as the UK and France) probably
come to mind. But a small, northern
European city is making a bid to put itself
on the map as a major start-up hub – and
with impressive results so far.

Better known for their sizeable system
of canals, absurd people-to-bike ratio
and attitude to work-life balance, it's
not as though the Dutch don't have a
history of excelling in business. This
new entrepreneurial era is a reflection
of the early 17th century, when the
pioneering nation established the first
stock exchange in 1602 and the famed
Dutch East India Company dominated
trade across the globe.

Four centuries later, the economy
is profiting from silicon rather than silk
and spices. The Netherlands' latest
regeneration began in the late 1990s,

with the establishment of start-ups
Booking.com and TomTom, two unicorns
(technology start-ups valued at more than
$1bn) that arose from the capital. At the
start of the new millennium the arrival of
Adyen, Gemalto and Catawiki reinforced
the nation's credentials as a home for
fledgling businesses. The Netherlands can
offer exemplary travel and logistics
infrastructure, proximity to European
markets, attractive business tax regulations
and, on top of that, the fact that English
is widely spoken. All this, plus a general
reputation for openness and liveability,
have made Amsterdam a magnet for
global companies: Netflix, Uber and Tesla
have all chosen the canal city for their
European headquarters.

The politician who played a leading
role in making the Netherlands Europe's
start-up hub is Neelie Kroes, the former
European commissioner for the digital
agenda. Appointed as the special envoy
for start-ups in 2014, she led the launch
of StartupDelta, an initiative to connect
government, start-ups, corporates, universities, research centres and investors. Amsterdam now lays claim to being the continent's best-connected and largest ecosystem for new technology businesses.

"Making money often doesn't seem to be the new entrepreneur's number-one priority; ideas – and harnessing them to make a better world – are of greater interest"

Kroes's successor, Prince Constantijn of the
Netherlands, has come to his new job with
even more ambitious plans. His challenge
is to push start-ups to scale-ups. "People
need to believe that they can grow really
big," he says. "What we are looking at is
not the café at the corner but the new
Starbucks. We have a few companies that
we call unicorns but they are very focused

on delivering. Once they launch an IPO
[an Initial Public Offering: the first sale
of stock by a company to the public],
those people and the money they made
will come back to the ecosystem. You will
start to see more of the entrepreneurs
who are starting to drive the system."

The new way of doing business –
casual, collaborative and light years from
traditional hierarchical structures – can
be seen in B Amsterdam, a 40,000 sq m
co-working space in the central business
district that is home to about 250
companies. "The idea is to create a buzz
and a physical space where you can bring
people together, to create a network of
sharing, mentoring and evolving," says
co-founder Guus Meulendijks. Last
year, in collaboration with the City of
Amsterdam, it launched BSSA (B Startup
School Amsterdam). The idea is to tackle
youth unemployment and a lack of talent
in the start-up arena by providing free
education and commercial matchmaking.

Further evidence of Amsterdam's
grand plans is the launch of Scale
(Startup City Alliance Europe). Major
hubs such as London, Berlin, Paris,
Barcelona, Helsinki, Stockholm, Rome,
Brussels, Oslo and Lisbon have already
signed up. The idea is to unite municipal
governments, corporations and institutions
to help companies link up with their
neighbouring markets.

The country's small population pushes
start-ups to think globally from the outset.
One of its best-known successes is large

file-sharing tool WeTransfer; following its conception in 2009 it is now used in 190 countries. Co-founder Nalden says: "Berlin is affordable, London has the capital and is often used as a hub of US-based venture capitals or enterprises, and we sit nicely in between the two. Now that the future of the EU is shifting this might be very positive for Amsterdam as we will definitely see some of that money moving here."

Despite the often-unthinkable sums to be made from ingenious start-ups, making money often doesn't seem to be the new entrepreneur's number-one priority; ideas – and harnessing them to make a better world – are of greater interest. An ethical example is the mobile-only challenger bank Bunq. In 2013, Ali Niknam founded the first greenfield bank (a start-up with no history in the field) to operate under a full Dutch banking licence in more than 35 years. "Our ideology is to make banking serve people again; we don't invest with your money and we don't trade your personal data," he says. The integrated banking app has been rolled out in Germany and Austria.

There are many more names to look out for in the future: Vandebron is a green-energy company connecting users directly with suppliers; StuDocu enables people to access and share study resources; and 3D Hubs provides an online 3D-printing service platform. Start-ups, it seems, will cease to emerge only when imagination and ambition run out. — (M)

ABOUT THE WRITER: Yoko Choy is a journalist and marketing consultant living between Amsterdam and Hong Kong. She enjoys the city's creativeness but sometimes finds it hard to balance Dutch plain-speaking with the Chinese imperative to "give face".

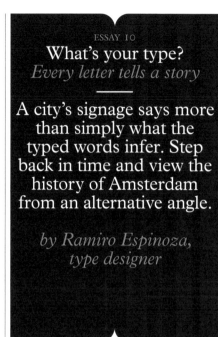

ESSAY 10
What's your type?
Every letter tells a story

___

A city's signage says more than simply what the typed words infer. Step back in time and view the history of Amsterdam from an alternative angle.

by Ramiro Espinoza, type designer

I'm a type designer: someone who earns a living designing fonts. It's an offbeat profession. Type designers can behave like eccentric astronomers or entomologists, focusing on the specimens no one else would even notice or rhapsodising about an unexpected find. But professional oddities aside, the fact is this: as a type designer I know how to interpret meanings and narratives encoded in letterforms.

So I'd like to invite you on a different kind of tour of Amsterdam: an exploration of the city's monumental lettering and hand-painted signs. Doesn't that sound slightly more tantalising than the usual tourist trail?

I promise you that fascinating stories lurk behind Amsterdam's humble letters.

Let's start with those famous bridges. Most of the iron bridges in the city centre feature cast nameplates (Oranjebrug, for example). The letters on these nameplates were designed by the municipality's Public Works department in about 1930. Their quirky design – a compelling mix of organic and geometric elements – originated in the aesthetic ideals championed by the Amsterdam School (*see pages 112 to 113*), a progressive and socially conscious group of architects who, between 1910 and 1930, designed iconic buildings and working-class housing estates.

"Whenever I see Rondo being used I can't help but remember with sadness that its designer died in Auschwitz in 1944"

Now these *Amsterdamse brugletters* (bridge letters) are celebrated as one of the strongest elements of Amsterdam's visual identity. The bridge-style lettering crops up in the logos of many businesses across the city and variations of this font now also appear on several concrete bridges throughout Amsterdam. The Blauwbrug over the Amstel River and the Vondelbrug (Van Baerlestraat over the Vondelpark) are fine examples of this carved relative of the bridge letter.

Moving on to the area around Centraal station, take a stroll down Haarlemmerstraat and its continuation Haarlemmerdijk. It's a pleasant walk along a retail strip, which grows more charming the further west you walk. If you pay close attention to the façades you'll find some intriguing examples of gothic (132 Haarlemmerstraat) and art nouveau (51 Haarlemmerstraat; 39 Haarlemmerdijk) signs painted on coloured tiles.

At 82 Haarlemmerstraat there is a hardware and paint shop called Evert Bruijnesteijn BV. Its logo is set in the typeface Rondo, originally designed by Stefan Schlesinger for the Tetterode Foundry. During the second half of the 20th century it was a popular font and can still be found in the branding of several Dutch companies. Whenever I see Rondo being used I can't help but remember with sadness that Schlesinger died in Auschwitz in 1944.

If you get as far as the Binnen Oranjestraat it's just a 15-minute walk to one of Amsterdam's most beautiful neighbourhoods: Jordaan. Once you're there I encourage you to pay attention to the centuries-old façades and look for the traditional Dutch *gevelstenen* (gable stones). These stone tablets (*see page 120*) emerged in the 16th century before house numbers came into use. *Gevelstenen* usually combine an image with a sentence or motto related to the profession of the person at that address. Although they didn't use a single typeface, many inscriptions share common features. Most employ a roman all-caps font with pointed angles and a strong character, which I find very handsome.

To end this typographic walk – considering that you're already in the Jordaan district – I advise you to seek out some examples of Amsterdam's pub lettering called the Amsterdamse Krulletter (*see page 121*). This decorative, curvy script was created in the mid-20th century by Jan Willem Joseph Visser, a sign-painter who used to work for the Amstel brewery.

Visser was inspired by the work of the Dutch Golden Age's calligraphy masters. As his style became popular among bar owners it was painted on the windows of dozens of Amsterdam pubs, becoming an important element of the old *bruin* café (brown café) aesthetic. The homely cafés Hegeraad (34 Noordermarkt), Chris (42 Bloemstraat), De Nieuwe Lelie (83 Nieuwe Leliestraat) and Rooie Nelis (101 Laurierstraat) are good starting points.

Settle into a cosy window spot in one of these cafés, order a glass of *genever* and stare out at the hand-painted letters. Soon you'll find that while sipping the fragrant liquor in front of the arching lettering, you'll catch a glimpse of an old Amsterdam that stubbornly resists the passage of time. — (M)

**Best 'bruine' cafés
with Krulletters**
—

01 **Café de Eland**
Cosy and quiet.
02 **Café 't Molentje**
Wood-panelled pub with
live music.
03 **Café de Twee Zwaantjes**
Venerated staple known for
folk singalongs.

ABOUT THE WRITER: Ramiro Espinoza specialised in type design at KABK in The Hague and the Plantin Institute of Typography in Antwerp. As well as contributing to design magazines he also runs the ReType Foundry, where he sells his own typefaces.

ESSAY 11

After dark
The night manager

Thanks to a little foresight and a creative approach, Amsterdammers have found a way to bridge their city's daytime and night-time economies.

by Mirik Milan, former night mayor

Amsterdam is such a liveable city. The rent is relatively low, the culture offering is unmatched (we have more museums per square mileage than any other city) and the nightlife is better than ever. My position as night mayor started as a voluntary one in 2012 but the role was first introduced in 2003 when new legislation to restrict pole dancing was introduced by city hall. There was public and commercial outcry over the disconnect between politicians and the people: it was their city and if politicians had no clue about what was going on in late-night culture then they shouldn't be introducing prohibitive laws about it.

That was the first time that left-wing politicians decided they needed someone to inform them about what was going on at night. The first night mayor was appointed and they began the night watch, writing a manifesto about the relationship between the night-time economy and culture. The idea was born in the Netherlands and Amsterdam was the first city to ensure that the night mayor wasn't just a title but a position that catalysed positive change for the city.

Today we are an independent NGO with a budget between €50,000 and €60,00 per year and a team of 20. This includes 12 advisers from different backgrounds such as clubs, festivals, culture and diversity, as well as safety and regulations. Our approach is to first find the vision and then influence legislation. A lot of people don't realise how big the industry that operates between 20.00 and 08.00 is. When you look at the electronic-music industry alone in the Netherlands, it has an annual turnover of €600m and creates 13,000 jobs.

On top of that, you have the immeasurable aspect of the culture: there is a lot of talent development happening in the nightlife industry. Elizabeth Currid wrote a book called *The Warhol Economy: How Fashion, Art, and Music Drive New York City* and this is precisely how I see nightlife in Amsterdam. The night is the time for the unexpected and a place to create. But if you want to explain this to policymakers you have to speak their language; this is why we call ourselves rebels in suits. We need to have both industry and city hall working together to make smart policy.

The most influential policy change we've helped create over the years is the introduction of 24-hour venues: there are

Legendary club venues

01 Melkweg
Dates back to the 1970s and one of the few open until 05.00.
02 Warehouse
A seminal hardcore venue (formerly Elementenstraat).
03 Gashouder
Large-scale raves in an old gas reserve.

now 10 clubs and bars across the city with a 24-hour licence. Venues such as De School, Radion and Shelter are multidisciplinary, with a bar, restaurant, gallery and work space for young creatives, as well as a nightclub, which all help fund other cultural endeavours. This, in turn, encourages a shared responsibility for the space. Although these sites may be a little way out, Amsterdammers deem it worth cycling 25 minutes to get there.

Amsterdam definitely has its own personality. It's a small city so it's possible to experience many great things all in one night. In the future I'd love to see contemporary art and late-night culture become more integrated. I think it could be fantastic for all 60 museums here to develop a strong relationship with 60 nightclubs. Although I won't be night mayor forever, my life goal is to elevate the quality of nightlife to the point where the royal ballet could be connected to an electronic-music show and that would be your night out.

The night is when our creative people meet and draw inspiration from each other and I know it's not for everybody. But in Amsterdam the scene is brimming with proactive, open-minded, forward-thinking people who have different opinions on diversity and inclusivity. I think society could learn a lot from what happens in our city after dark. — (M)

ABOUT THE WRITER: Mirik Milan has worked as a club promoter, creative director and from 2012 to 2018 as night mayor of Amsterdam. He was the capital's spokesman for all things nightlife and successfully built a bridge between municipality, business owners and residents.

ESSAY 12

Full circle
Dutch food gets a makeover

Worried you'll go hungry for quality food in Amsterdam? Today there's something for everyone in this diverse city – including excellent local fare – but it's true that this hasn't always been the case.

by Vicky Hampton, food writer

History is said to be cyclical and the story of the Netherlands' cuisine is no exception. While the Dutch Golden Age brought a bounty of exotic spices and fruit to the country from across its extensive empire, the 20th century saw a return to the simple diet of potatoes, cheap cuts of meat, fish and local vegetables that Amsterdammers had previously been used to. It's not for nothing that the Dutch are known for their frugality; being thrifty has proven useful in many aspects of life (very few Dutch have credit card debt) but it doesn't do much for the reputation of the national cuisine.

So it's not overly surprising that when I moved to Amsterdam from the UK in 2006, I fell in love with the city but not with its food. Lacking a national identity for its cuisine that didn't extend much beyond chips with mayo and the rather unidentifiable filling inside *bitterballen*, restaurants had turned to France for their inspiration. In the mid-2000s almost all the best examples served classic French cuisine, with a handful of decent Italian restaurants thrown in the mix. Dutch institutions such as Greetje were (and still are) offering traditional Lowlands' cuisine but, despite doing it rather well, there was hardly a broad appetite for the hearty and strangely named dishes: "pigeon's hangover", anyone?

Then something changed. As Amsterdam's chefs started to travel, the city's restaurant scene became as diverse as its visitors. Today diners can enjoy everything from Japanese *kaiseki* to Mexican tacos and Ethiopian *injera*. French fare fell out of fashion and Dutch chefs looked further and further afield for inspiration. I could pen an entire book about the diversity of cuisine in a city that calls itself home to more nationalities than any other metropolis on the planet (yes, including London and New York) but this is about the cycle of history, so I'll stick to topic.

True to form, more than a decade later we've come full circle once again: French food is back in vogue. Top chef Ron Blaauw, known for being on the cutting edge of culinary trends, opened Ron Gastrobar Paris in 2016. It's a buzzing bistro-style restaurant that transports you straight to the City of Light with its retro *oeufs* mimosa and steak tartare. Meanwhile, Auberge Jean & Marie has opened in the hip De Pijp area, proving that fine wine and frogs' legs are popular even among millennials (at least, those who can afford them).

"Dutch institutions like Greetje were offering traditional cuisine but there was hardly a broad appetite for the strangely named dishes: 'pigeon's hangover', anyone?"

But more important still is the positive turn that Dutch food itself has taken. In some cases this applies only to the ingredients; in others it applies to the style of cooking. Many Dutch chefs (just like most chefs worldwide) have long been of the opinion that the closer the provenance of the produce, the better-tasting the dish. Which is why restaurant De Kas (*see page 35*), housed in a greenhouse that produces the majority of the vegetables, fruit and herbs used in its kitchen, has already stood the test of time for more than a decade. Likewise, Marius has been serving a "market menu" of four fixed courses, depending on what's fresh and in season at the market, since the early 2000s.

Newer restaurants in Amsterdam have taken things one step further. Guts & Glory (*see page 27*) uses a related concept in which the menu focuses on chapters (an animal, for example, or a particular cuisine) that change every couple of months. In the east of the city, Eetbar Wilde Zwijnen has been serving small sharing plates of modern Dutch seasonal fare, such as lamb belly and white asparagus, since 2015.

Two restaurants, however, have really raised the stakes. Choux (*see page 36*) is nestled under the railway line close to Centraal station; one look at the menu shows how serious chef Merijn van Berlo is about Dutch produce. *Stoofpeer* (spiced, stewed Gieser Wildeman pears) and *zuurkool* (Holland's answer to sauerkraut) feature in one dish. *Monniksbaard* (a succulent plant that grows in salty coastal areas) and shellfish feature in another. The wine selection is equally interesting. While they may not be Dutch (wine is produced in the south of the country but tends to be expensive for the level of quality), they are organic.

Meanwhile, Restaurant Breda (named after a small city in the country's south) knocked the socks off Amsterdam's food scene in 2016. A simple plate of charred runner beans with a mint purée took me straight back to my parents' garden when I was a child. The refined yet elegant flavours continued throughout the five-course dinner, right through to the sorrel granita, which was grassy and spiked with ginger. Traditional Dutch food it is not but Breda is bringing back local ingredients within an international context – and making it work spectacularly.

A decade after moving to Amsterdam I can honestly say that I'm now as enamoured with its cuisine as I was with its canals all those years ago. I'm curious about what the next decade has in store; I can only hope that we're about to enter the Golden Age of Dutch cuisine. — (M)

Picks for dining out
—
01 **Choux**
Locally sourced food and organic wine.
02 **Breda**
Creative, accomplished and modern Dutch cooking.
03 **Eetbar Wilde Zwijnen**
Small sharing plates of Dutch fare.

ABOUT THE WRITER: Vicky Hampton is a British-born food writer who's been living in Amsterdam since 2006. She runs the website *amsterdamfoodie.nl* and writes for several publications and guidebooks. She recently applied for Dutch citizenship.

Culture
—— Dutch mastery

With thousands of exhibits packed within its walls, the Rijksmuseum alone has enough cultural riches to make a capital city blush. That it's just one of Amsterdam's jewels means you'll never be far from somewhere enchanting to explore.

The city's art history is something to be proud of and investment has built new museums and given facelifts to others. But if you fancy sidestepping the crowds swarming around the Old Masters there's a vibrant modern-art scene to explore outside the Museumplein. In this section we list the small galleries, photography studios and modern-art houses leading the way.

Amsterdam's liberal reputation is well known and that rebellious streak is apparent in its small theatres, cutting-edge art projects, eclectic music venues and independent cinemas. We'll direct you to the best, as well as to free classical concerts at Het Concertgebouw. The 17th century may have been the Golden Age but culturally the capital is still shining bright.

Museums
Art and artefacts

① Rijksmuseum, Oud-Zuid
The full monty

What will you see when visiting the Rijksmuseum? Oh, you know: sculptures from the Middle Ages; 18th-century decorative arts; a bit of everything from the 19th century; 20th-century minimalism and modernism; the zero movement; romanesques; the baroque; mannerism; gothic art; the renaissance; rococo; classicism; the Italianate; art nouveau; impressionism; Romanticism; bronzes; still lifes; Asian art; artefacts from 11th-century churches; Vermeer; Van Gogh; Rembrandt; silverware; Samurai helmets; ceremonial swords; Meissen porcelain; Delft pottery; a tiny potty; a lead-booted diving suit; models of ships; lighthouses; and shoes.

"Less is more," says director Taco Dibbits. Less? There are about 8,000 objects in 80 galleries chosen from one million pieces in the collection. "It was really a case of 'kill your darlings'," he says of the choice. Luckily, he still has 992,000 darlings left to play with.
1 Museumstraat, 1071 XX
+ 31 (0)20 674 7000
rijksmuseum.nl

②
Stedelijk Museum, Oud-Zuid
Make it modern

The Stedelijk Museum has been a central part of the city's cultural landscape since 1874. Its curation focuses on contemporary and modern art (primarily from the 1920s and onwards) and shows big names such as Chagall, Rothko and Lichtenstein, as well as up-and-coming artists.

Two major renovations have given room to allow the gallery's scope to expand. These include the 2012 "bathtub" extension and the 1950s wing, which was built to house works from Amsterdam-based artists.
10 Museumplein, 1071 DJ
+31 (0)20 573 2911
stedelijk.nl

De Stijl movement

The distinct primary-colour patchwork of the De Stijl movement has its origins in the Netherlands. Dutch painters Theo van Doesburg and Piet Mondrian founded the publication *De Stijl* (meaning *The Style*) in 1917 as a mouthpiece for their ideas on art and utopian society. It led to the abstract movement, with its use of vertical and horizontal geometry.

The movement's reach extended to literature, music, typography, industrial design and most notably architecture with the rise of the International Style in the 1920s and 1930s.

In 2017 the Stedelijk Museum marked De Stijl's 100-year anniversary with a major retrospective. There is also a permanent exhibition.

❸
Van Gogh Museum, Oud-Zuid
A masterpiece for masterpieces

This is one of the most visited galleries in the world so battling crowds is inevitable. The museum houses the largest collection of the Dutch post-impressionist painter's work, including "Sunflowers", "Almond Blossom", "The Bedroom" and "Potato Eaters".

A new entrance designed by Dutch architect Hans van Heeswijk was added in 2015 to help with the flow of people. It sits in stark contrast to Gerrit Rietveld's 1973 De Stijl-inspired original.
6 Museumplein, 1071 DJ
+31 (0)20 570 5200
vangoghmuseum.nl

④
Eye Filmmuseum, Noord
Movie buff heaven

In 2012 the Filmmuseum relocated from Vondelpark to its new distinctive home on the IJ harbourfront, directly opposite Centraal station. Dusting off its collection dedicated to the world of film, it's now a modern shrine for silver-screen aficionados. "We want to show a wide spectrum of the art of film, including great retrospectives from Kubrick to Fellini but also more obscure and experimental work," says Sandra den Hamer, director of Eye. The exhibitions are shown in the versatile and expansive space and the cinema's four screens offer a mix of avant garde and arthouse films, Dutch classics and Hollywood blockbusters.

The wide-ranging programme also includes weekly series such as *Eye On Art*, a partnership with the city's top galleries, and cinema concerts, presenting silent films with live music. The building is home to a top-notch gift shop, selling everything from vintage film posters (*see page 66*) to Lolita sunglasses and wine from Francis Ford Coppola's vineyard. There's also a restaurant and bar.
1 IJpromenade, 1031 KT
+ 31 (0)20 589 1400
eyefilm.nl

Public galleries
Art for all

❶
Kunstverein, Jordaan
Experimental art

Toronto-born Maxine Kopsa co-founded Kunstverein in 2009 as a platform for artists she considered to be historically overlooked. The intimate space is near the bigger commercial galleries in Jordaan but has a more distinctive and experimental tone. Kunstverein's roster of lectures, screenings and performances doesn't follow the traditional format: exhibitions are rarely limited to pictures on walls, instead often spilling over into books and sometimes furniture.

Previous shows have featured works from Israeli choreographer Noa Eshkol and British constructivism maverick Marlow Moss. The gallery also has an independent publishing arm and sells print publications that will appeal to graphic-design enthusiasts and offbeat-art lovers.
28 Hazenstraat, 1016 SR
+ 31 (0)20 331 3203
kunstverein.nl

②
Huis Marseille, Centrum
Quiet location

Amsterdam's first photography museum opened its doors in 1999 in a unique setting. Huis Marseille's two 17th-century canal houses might not look much from the outside but hiding within are a library, garden and photo exhibitions hung in two princely Golden Age-era rooms.

Less crowded and more serene than Fotografiemuseum Amsterdam (Foam), this is a better option for exploring high-quality photographs in great detail. The gallery closes one week before all new exhibitions so be sure to check.
401 Keizersgracht, 1016 EK
+ 31 (0)20 531 8989
huismarseille.nl

Pakt, Eastern Docklands
Emerging talent

Art historian Nienke Vijlbrief
and artist Rob van de Werdt
decided to join forces in 2003 and
create a space to give art-academy
graduates and emerging talent a
platform. At the time, surging rents
in the city were causing artists to
depart for Rotterdam and Berlin
so local government began offering
affordable studio space, which the
pair snapped up.

  "We think it's important for
younger artists to be given the
means, space and time to develop
and show new work," says Vijlbrief.
"Pakt functions as a bridge
between art academies, artist-run
initiatives and the established
galleries and museums." It's
housed in a warehouse in the
Eastern Docklands area, which is
experiencing steady regeneration.
The duo look for artists who fully
explore the capacity of the space.
*53 Zeeburgerpad, 1019 AB
+ 31 (0)65 427 0879
pakt.nu*

W139, Centrum
Risky business

In 1979 young artists Guus van
der Werf, Marianne Kronenberg,
Martha Crijns, Reinout Weydom
and Ad de Jong transformed an
old theatre in the red-light district
into an anti-establishment space
to show their works to friends. By
1990 it was a bona fide gallery with
a motto of "room for risk".

  Today W139 remains an artist-
run gallery with a rebellious streak.
Its exhibitions, which feature both
Dutch and international talent, may
be too out-there for some but for
hardcore art fans it's a window into
1980s Amsterdam counterculture.
*139 Warmoesstraat, 1012 JB
+ 31 (0)20 622 9434
w139.nl*

Out of town

Following funding problems,
De Appel, one of the city's best
curators of contemporary art,
moved out of the city centre
to Westlandgracht. It's worth
the journey as exhibitions
here rarely disappoint and the
graduates it champions often
go on to achieve great things.
deappel.nl

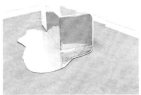

⑤
Het Hem, Zaandam
Art, music and more

Housed in a former munitions factory in the far northwest of the city, Het Hem is a vast multidisciplinary art centre comprising an exhibition space, a media library, two restaurants and an underground "audiophile listening bar" that hosts DJs from around the world.

Opened in 2019, it hosts resident curators on a three-month basis who are tasked with creating work to go on display. Past participants have included musician Nicolas Jaar and the founders of Dutch streetwear brand Patta.
1 Warmperserij, 1505 RI.
+ 31 (0)75 710 0073
hethem.nl

❶
Annet Gelink Gallery, Jordaan
Making a point

There's a cluster of commercial galleries in the south of Jordaan, where Annet Gelink Gallery has been since 2000. Founder Annet Gelink and director Floor Wullems have built a stable of talent, mostly discovered at the Rijksakademie.

Represented artists include Amsterdam resident Maria Barnas, Japanese film director Meiro Koizumi and Israeli artist Yael Bartana; there's also Croatian David Maljkovic, who explores the cultural and social heritage of his home country. The gallery's oeuvre is hard-hitting and often political.
187-189 Laurierstraat, 1016 PL.
+ 31 (0)20 330 2066
annetgelink.com

②
Ellen de Bruijne Projects, Centrum
Cutting-edge artists

This contemporary-art gallery
opened in 1999 with a rebellious
social and subtly feminist voice.
Over the years it has resisted the
pull of the mainstream and still
feels in tune with the innovative
subculture of the city, focusing
on performance art, installations
and more.

Still-life photographer and
Amsterdam resident Uta Eisenreich,
and Bulgarian performance artist
Zhana Ivanova, are among its
roll call of conceptual artists.
372 Singel, 1016 AH
+ 31 (0)64 948 5207
edbprojects.com

③
Grimm, Centrum
Twice as good

Showing contemporary art since
2005, Jorg Grimm's gallery has
rapidly gained a reputation on
the global art stage. His roster of
increasingly international artists has
included Charles Avery, Matthew
Day Jackson and Daniel Richter.

Since 2010 Grimm has been
based on the pretty Frans Halsstraat
in De Pijp and in 2017 opened a
second space in De 9 Straatjes. Both
the industrial space in De Pijp and
the charming 17th-century canal
house complement the vast range
of exhibited work.
26 Frans Halsstraat, 1072 BR;
241 Keizersgracht, 1016 EA
+ 31 (0)20 675 2465
grimmgallery.com

Apologies if we're looking a bit miffed

④
Galerie Fons Welters, Jordaan
The godfather

As one of the oldest and arguably the most powerful, Fons Welters is the grandfather of commercial galleries and one whose eccentric house is always worth a visit. Art wasn't the obvious career path for him: he started out helping on his father's farm before moving to the bright lights in the riotous 1980s.

For more than three decades his gallery has grown on the national and international stages and helped shape the commercial offerings in the city. Welters has a particular knack for finding compelling sculpture and installation artists.
140 Bloemstraat, 1016 LJ
+ 31 (0)20 423 3046
fonswelters.nl

Off-the-wall offerings
Weird and wonderful

①
De School, De Baarsjes
Independent venue

This multi-use space comes from the team behind Trouw, an iconic venue in an old printing factory that closed in 2015. "When we were looking for a site we cycled around looking for somewhere that we could give a new dimension to," says managing director Ernst Mertens.

When the team came across a former technical college they knew they'd found their location; they turned it into a club, restaurant, art space and gym in 2016. All of the programming is independently curated so it remains current.
1 Doctor Jan van Breemenstraat, 1056 AB
+ 31 (0)20 737 3197
deschoolamsterdam.nl

Give it a go

Eddie The Eagle Museum is a not-for-profit artist-run collective that drums up bizarre and brilliant content. Named after the UK ski jumper, it's about the art of trying, from performance through to photography.
eddietheeaglemuseum.com

②
Pakhuis de Zwijger, Eastern
Docklands
Talking shop

Pakhuis de Zwijger opened in
2006 in a modernist warehouse in
Eastern Docklands. The not-for-
profit organisation hosts debates,
discussions and think-tanks on
everything from quality of life,
innovation and technology to
the relationship between the
government and citizens.
   Talks are usually in Dutch but
some are in English depending
on the guests and topics covered.
With more than 600 events
annually, it's a dynamic place to
drop by to engage in a lively chat.
179 Piet Heinkade, 1019 HC
+ 31 (0)20 624 6380
dezwijger.nl

Live venues
Face the action

❶
Muziekgebouw aan 't IJ and
Bimhuis, Eastern Docklands
Moving music

Two of the Netherlands' best
music venues reside side by side.
The award-winning buildings
by Danish firm 3XN are home to
contemporary and classical-music
hall the Muziekgebouw aan 't IJ
and Bimhuis, the place for jazz.
   Muziekgebouw has movable
walls, floors and ceilings that adapt
to suit musical styles, while the
Bimhuis's amphitheatre hall is
more intimate.
Muziekgebouw aan 't IJ:
1 Piet Heinkade, 1019 BR
+ 31 (0)20 788 2000; muziekgebouw.
nl
Bimhuis:
3 Piet Heinkade, 1019 BR

② Het Concertgebouw, Oud-Zuid
Top of the classical

Since hosting its first concert in 1888, this Amsterdam institution has become one of the world's most respected halls: Gustav Mahler, Richard Strauss, Louis Armstrong and Cecilia Bartoli have all graced its stage. You can watch a symphonic orchestra in the majestic Main Hall, opt for chamber music in the Recital Hall or settle in the intimate Choir Hall. Even if you're not a seasoned enthusiast, it's worth a visit. On Wednesdays the Concertgebouw hosts free lunchtime concerts.
10 Concertgebouwplein, 1071 LN
+31 (0)20 671 8345
concertgebouw.nl

③ Paradiso, Centrum
Young at heart

Known for its eclectic mix of shows, Paradiso is a musical mainstay on the edge of the canal ring. A converted church dating back to the 19th century, it opened its doors as a music venue in 1968.

Since then it's been a centre for counter and youth culture. From punk in the 1970s to raves in the 1990s, acts such as The Cure, The Roots, Amy Winehouse and Lenny Kravitz have all performed here. Paradiso also hosts wider cultural projects such as fashion shows, film screenings and lectures.
6-8 Weteringschans, 1017 SG
+31 (0)20 626 4521
paradiso.nl

④ Frascati Theater, Centrum
Acting up

The Frascati Theater dates back to the 1580s when it was a haunt for intellectuals in the bustling trade district. Its name came later, from a coffeehouse that opened within the venue in 1810. A 1,500-capacity ballroom was added, drawing in audiences for live vaudeville comedies and kickstarting the area's entertainment scene.

Today the Frascati has four theatre spaces: three at 63 Nes and another at 71 Nes. It's a centre for live performance, hosts more than 700 shows annually and is a breeding ground for new talent.
63 Nes, 1012 KD
+31 (0)20 626 6866
frascatitheater.nl

①
Filmtheater De Uitkijk, Centrum
Cinematic heritage

When De Uitkijk opened in 1912, moviegoers would buy their tickets from a booth outside before entering the single-screen theatre. A café and foyer have been added but you can still see the original ticket machine on display.

Entrepreneur Bart Lubbers bought the cinema in 2007 and placed its programming in the hands of the same student organisation that looks after Kriterion (*see page 102*). A mainly European bill offers themed seasons, wine evenings and silent films with live music.
452 Prinsengracht, 1017 KE
+ 31 (0)20 223 2416
uitkijk.nl

Amsterdam on film

01 **Diamonds Are Forever, 1971:** Amsterdam makes a cameo in the sixth and last James Bond film to star Sean Connery when tourists on a boat witness a body being pulled from the Amstel River near the Magere Brug. Be sure to note Bond's mistake: the secret agent, disguised as a Dutch diamond smuggler, greets his enemy with the German "*Guten abend*" instead of the Dutch "*Goedenavond*".

02 **Turkish Delight, 1973:** Directed by Paul Verhoeven, this turbulent love story, based on the erotic 1969 novel by Jan Wolkers, received an Oscar nomination for best foreign-language film. Set within the bohemian art world in Amsterdam, it is a raw depiction of a turbulent love story.

03 **Amsterdamned, 1988:** This Dutch cult horror film directed by Dick Maas turns Amsterdam's historic canal ring into a hellish nightmare. After several bodies are found floating in the city's waterways, a detective discovers something sinister lurking beneath the surface.

04 **Black Book, 2006:** Two decades after leaving the Netherlands, renowned director Paul Verhoeven (*see above*) returned from Hollywood to make this big-budget thriller. Based on true events, it tells the story of a young Jewish woman who becomes a spy for the resistance during the Second World War. Pivotal scenes were shot in Amsterdam; at the time of its release it was the most expensive Dutch film ever made.

2 Tuschinski, Centrum
Ornate beauty

Polish businessman Abraham Icek Tuschinski first became mesmerised by the silver screen after designing the uniforms for cinema porters. Not long after, he commissioned the construction of a spate of film theatres across the Netherlands, the most prominent of which was his eponymous masterpiece in the capital. Doors opened in 1921 and the interior design combined a beautiful mix of Amsterdam School, art nouveau and art deco styles.

Painstakingly preserved and now owned by Pathé, the Tuschinski is still considered one of Europe's most ornate and decadent cinemas. The main 740-seat auditorium plays the blockbusters while the five smaller theatres show a more independent roster. To soak up the full rich history, ask about the audio tour.
*26-28 Reguliersbreestraat, 1017 CN
pathe.nl*

The gallery gave me a right earful for doing this

The Movies, Jordaan
History maker

Like Filmtheater De Uitkijk
(*see page 100*), The Movies began
screening in 1912, making it one
of the oldest cinemas in town (it's
rumoured that the original art deco
interior inspired Tuschinski). It
started off with a single screen but
in 1971 the owners acquired space
in the neighbouring buildings and
expanded to four screening rooms.

In 1989 another room was
added, along with a restaurant next
to the entrance. The programming
now finds a happy medium
between blockbuster and arthouse.
161 Haarlemmerdijk, 1013 KH
+ 31 (0)20 638 6016
themovies.nl

③ Kriterion, De Plantage
Student beginnings

This former Jewish workers' union
building was transformed into a
cinema by a group of students in
1945. During the Second World
War they were actively involved
in the resistance movements
and afterwards they founded the
Kriterion as a way of supporting
other students, employing them
to make studies more affordable.

Kriterion is still student-run and
at the countercultural heart of the
city. It shows edgy arthouse films,
eclectic documentaries and Oscar
winners. The café charges are
modest and it hosts live music.
170 Roetersstraat, 1018 WE
+ 31 (0)20 623 1708
kriterion.nl

Media round-up
What to read and listen to

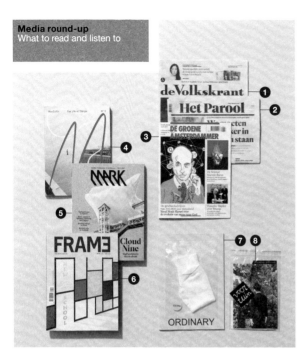

Athenaeum Nieuwscentrum,
Centrum
Alternative newsstand

Kiosk culture isn't big in the city;
instead newsstands tend to come
in the form of bookshop-kiosks.
The Nieuwscentrum at the
Athenaeum Boekhandel, one of the
Netherlands' biggest independent
bookshops (*see page 62*), is the
city's best-known spot for buying
the latest copies of your favourite
publications. It stocks international
magazines covering everything
from current affairs to cooking.
The staff are happy to share their
knowledge about anything going
on in the world of print.
14 Spui, 1012 XA
+31 (0)20 514 1460
athenaeum.nl

Radio

01 Red Light Radio: This
online station playing
international music
broadcasts from the
heart of the red-light
district – a window onto
Oudekerksplein allows
passers-by to peer in. It
was founded in 2010 and
was awarded the Mixcloud
Best Online Radio Station
in 2015.
redlightradio.net

02 BNR: For opinion and
reportage on political,
business and financial
news while in the capital,
tune into Business Nieuws
Radio on wavelength
101.8 FM. All the
programming is in Dutch.
bnr.nl

03 Salto: This open-access
broadcaster is run out of
the same building as
Pakhuis de Zwijger (*see
page 98*) and offers seven
different stations including
WereldFM, which often
has English-language
programming.
salto.nl

①
Magazines, citywide
The printed word

Amsterdam's independent
magazine and newspaper scene
is thriving. ❶ *De Volkskrant* is
a quality national daily; for a
slightly more left-leaning read,
❷ *Het Parool* is the most popular
local newspaper and was named
European newspaper of the year in
2016 (it's a daily that's published
in the afternoon). For in-depth
analysis of current affairs look
to ❸ *De Groene Amsterdammer*.
It's the Netherlands' esteemed
left-leaning magazine with thought-
provoking articles on society; it
has an aesthetic similar to that of
The New Yorker.
   A range of insightful English-
language publications have also hit
newsstands in recent years. Pick
up a copy of ❹ *MacGuffin*, the
winner of the magazine-of-the-year
award at the 2016 Stack Awards, to
find out about the life of ordinary
objects (such as a window, rope
or sink,) and stories about their
purpose and design.

❺ *Mark* focuses on modern
architecture, covering "starchitects
to new talent alike". The team
behind it also publish ❻ *Frame*:
a leading publication about interior
design that covers everything from
retail spaces to offices.
   The conceptual photography
magazine ❼ *Ordinary* explores
one seemingly mundane object
per issue but asks artists to send
in their "extraordinary" take
on the object. ❽ *Voortuin* is an
interesting example of artist-run
experimental publishing.

Monocle 24
———
It would be remiss not to
mention Monocle's own
radio station, which features
programmes ranging from
daily news to our design
show *Section D*. Listen online
at *monocle.com/radio* or
download the podcasts on
iTunes or SoundCloud.

Design and architecture
—— Sites to behold

Amsterdam's architecture dates back to the 14th century and when you imagine the city it's hard not to think solely in terms of canals, bridges and windmills. But the scope of design in the Dutch capital is wider and more diverse than the postcards might have you believe.

The brick-heavy work of the Amsterdam School, as espoused by Eduard Cuypers and his acolytes, is of particular interest, blending expressionism with art deco and art nouveau. At the same time, members of the movement were careful to apply socialist ideals that buildings should benefit all, not just the elite.

A respect for the city's architectural history has also led to the repurposing of structures that would otherwise have lain idle, themselves becoming a symbol of the city's pleasing juxtaposition of old and new. And there's plenty of modern and contemporary design to catch the eye too, from brutalist accommodation blocks to innovative solutions to the city's housing shortage.

Amphibious architecture
High and dry

①
REM Eiland, Noord
Rigged up as a restaurant

Standing on 12-metre-tall stilts, the red-and-white chequered REM Eiland was erected in 1964 and then towed 9km offshore into the North Sea where it was anchored to the seabed. Its purpose was to house the pirate broadcasting station Radio and TV Noordzee but after government objections the station was dismantled by the Royal Dutch Navy a few months later. It eventually resumed broadcast as a legal station and was on air until 2006, when it was again dismantled.

In 2011 the boxy three-storey structure took up a new residence in the IJ harbour just north of the city and opened as a restaurant. It still features the original footbridges, signal lights and lifeboat, while the former helipad is now a terrace offering great (if windswept) views back over the city from ust over 20 metres up.
45-2 Haparandadam, 1013 AK
+ 31 (0)20 688 5501
remeiland.com

②
Silodam, Centrum
Housing block

Silodam was inspired by the 19th
and 20th-century grain silos on the
docks of Oude Houthaven just to
the northwest of Centraal station.
In 1995, Rotterdam-based studio
MVRDV – also responsible for the
Hermès shop and Tennisclub
IJburg (*see page 124*) – was
commissioned to design a dense
living complex in the empty port.
Finished in 2003, the monumental
building looks like a stack of
shipping containers servicing
the surrounding silos.

The site houses 157 commercial
and residential units of varying
sizes, occupied by a cross-section
of financial categories (and also,
therefore, of Amsterdam's society).
MVRDV created internal streets and
central shared spaces, including
a restaurant, library and viewing
deck. There's also a small harbour
for residents to moor their boats.
Tours can be booked in advance.
Silodam, 1013 AW

③
Kraanspoor, Noord
Glazed look

Dreamed up by Trude Hooykaas,
founder of OTH Architecten, on a
bicycle ride (how very Dutch) in
1997, Kraanspoor faced numerous
roadblocks, including objections
from city hall. The 270-metre-
long glass office building took a
decade to complete and appears
to float three metres above a
decommissioned crane track on
the IJ river.

Hooykaas wanted to preserve
the area's industrial heritage while
giving it a new lease on life. The
building's façade is a wraparound
transparent second skin of movable
glass louvres that afford spectacular
views of the IJ river.
Kraanspoor, 1033 SE

④
Steigereiland, IJburg
Floating houses

With the city's housing shortage,
architects have been looking to
the water, developing practical
but good-looking floating homes.
Nearly 75 of them now dot the
artificial island cluster of IJburg
in the city's east. A network of
aluminium-surfaced jetties work as
footpaths and create a link between
the two and three-storey dwellings,
which range from social housing to
high-end abodes.

One cluster was designed by
Marlies Rohmer Architects, using
glass and synthetic materials that
resemble steel. The base is a hollow
cement cube, which is poured in
one go and takes into consideration
heavy pieces of furniture such as
pianos or bathtubs (a thicker slab of
concrete on the opposite side acts
as a counterweight). Once finished,
the houses are pulled along the
canals by barge to their destination.
Haringbuisdijk, 1086 VA
rohmer.nl

①
Canteen Building,
Eastern Docklands
Lofty ideals

As the name suggests, this was once
the canteen building for the now
defunct Royal Dutch Steamboat
Company – but new life was
breathed into the site in the early
1990s. The city council divided
the original space into eight loft
apartments, which it sold off for
symbolic sums to artist squatters.
 "We used old ship ladders to
provide an individual entrance for
each loft," says Koen Crabbendam
of Casa Architecten, who worked on
the initial brief. The artists renovated
the lofts themselves and owned the
properties under the condition that
they did not sell them for the first
10 years. Once the decade was up,
some of the properties soon went
for more than €1m.
1-15 Levantplein, 1019 MA

②
Rijksmuseum, Oud-Zuid
Refreshing the past

Ten years of renovations to Pierre
Cuypers' 1885 neo-gothic building
were completed in 2013; the main
hall is now an open courtyard by
Seville architects Cruz and Ortiz.
"There's so much light now, it's
a whole different mentality," says
gallery director Taco Dibbits.
Teams dug beneath sea level to
find more space and height for the
glass-roofed courtyard. "In the
Netherlands as soon as you put
a spade in the ground you need a
sailor, not a builder," adds Dibbits,
referencing the trouble with
building on reclaimed land.
 Now a concave tier of
Portuguese stone is overlooked by
a pair of towering new minimalist
porticos nudging up to the walls
of Cuypers' outspoken original.
The interior design, lighting and
staging of works was refreshed by
Frenchman Jean-Michel Wilmotte.
1 Museumstraat, 1071 XX
+ 31 (0)20 674 7000
rijksmuseum.nl

Ok you lot, you're
going to have to
breathe in

④
Het Scheepvaartmuseum,
Eastern Docklands
Top of the charts

Daniël Stalpaert, who also
designed the town hall (now the
royal palace), used his trademark
austere classical style for Het
Scheepvaartmuseum (The
National Maritime Museum). Built
as a naval warehouse in 1656, it
opened as a museum in 1973 and
was renovated from 2007 to 2011;
it was during this time that its
courtyard was roofed with 1,200
pieces of glass. The design was
inspired by compass lines on old
mapping charts, with LEDs placed
on each of the 868 "knots".
1 Kattenburgerplein, 1018 KK
+ 31 (0)20 523 2222
hetscheepvaartmuseum.nl

③
Gebouw 27E Marineterrein, Oost
Military planning

Dutch architecture bureau SLA
was tasked with transforming this
former military academy into
a setting fit to host the EU Council
during the Netherlands' presidency
back in 2016. Before that, the
13-hectare marine base had been
closed for more than 300 years.
  "There was a lot of mystery
surrounding this site, particularly
since it's right in the city centre,"
says Peter Van Assche, lead
designer at bureau SLA. The façade
was redesigned, each window
gaining oversized wooden louvres
abstractly representing European
flags. Spread out over three
floors, the building's large, open
spaces are now used as various
types of workspaces that are either
open to the public or rented out
to start-ups.
Marineterrein, 5 Kattenburgerstraat,
1018 JA
+ 31 (0)20 261 3656
marineterrein.nl

⑤
Stedelijk Museum, Oud-Zuid
Added extras

AW Weissman's Stedelijk Museum was completed in the Dutch neo-renaissance style in 1895 but various additions have been made to it over the years. The most ambitious was finished in 2012 by Benthem Crouwel Architects and took the form of a large white-and-glass wing known affectionately as the *badkuip* (bathtub).

"We wanted our design to include an urban-planning solution," says Mels Crouwel, founding partner at Benthem Crouwel. To achieve this the team reoriented the main entrance by 180 degrees to face Museumplein. "In doing so it created an active, common ground for the first time between all the square's cultural spaces," adds Crouwel.
10 Museumplein, 1071 DJ
+31 (0)20 573 2911
stedelijk.nl

Key players

The city is a hotbed for graphic-design talent and the Stedelijk Museum has brought some big-industry names into its fold over the years. Alumni include Wim Crouwel, who designed the museum's branding from 1963 to 1985, and typographer Willem Sandberg.
stedelijk.nl

Residential
Living legends

❶
The Pyramids, Westerpark
Three sides to every storey

The Pyramids are the highlight of Marcanti-eiland's redevelopment, started in the 1980s. Finished in 2006 by Soeters van Eldonk Architecten, these 50-metre-tall triangles imitate the shape of the industrial district and tap into HP Berlage's vision of the Amsterdam School.

The towers take the form of traditional gables, their stepped sides doubling as terraces, and house 82 apartments also designed by Soeters van Eldonk. The Pyramids' compact form allows for a large square on the half-sunken roof of an extensive garage, finished with ventilation pipes inspired by old-fashioned chimneys.
Jan van Galenstraat, 1051 KE

De Oude Kerk

It may not be as grandiose as gothic cathedrals elsewhere but De Oude Kerk is nonetheless impressive (and also the oldest building in Amsterdam). Wood was the primary material used during construction to ensure that the foundation wouldn't overload and sink: a very real concern for a city built on peat swamps. The church was consecrated at the beginning of the 14th century and operated until 1951, when it was closed due to concerns about the integrity of the foundations.

Extensive restoration took place between 1955 and 1979, and again between 1994 and 1998. Today Oude Kerk is home to an art institution that allows installation artists to create works that fit the soaring wooden ceilings and cracked stone floorspace.
oudekerk.nl

②
Nieuwendammerdijk, Noord
Triumphs in timber

These distinctive pretty houses, lining a long and narrow street in Noord, tell the history of a small village on the IJ river. They date back to the 16th century and were made of wood (unlike the typical Amsterdam stone canal houses) to ensure the dyke could hold their weight.

Constructed during the golden age of shipbuilding, trade and maritime transport, the embellished abodes were the homes of captains, fishermen, ferrymen and lock-keepers, not to mention wealthy families (number 202-204 was built for shipbuilding magnate de Vries Lentsch). The neoclassical houses at numbers 300 and 308 were home to doctor Johann Georg Mezger, one of the founders of physiotherapy. Princess Sophia of Nassau, wife of the Swedish prince and later King Oscar II, gave him land in Nieuwendam to thank him for treating her oldest son.
Nieuwendammerdijk, 1023 BT

Tricks of the trade
———
Visit the Museum Van Loon to see how the merchants lived in the golden era of trade. The Van Loon family (of Dutch East-India Company descent) has lived here since 1884 and opened part of the residence in 1973 to share its private collection with the public.
museumvanloon.nl

③
Betondorp, Oost
Concrete craftsmanship

This brutalist neighbourhood of 900 minimalist, art deco houses in the city's south was built in the 1920s as part of a construction experiment to address the country's rising brick prices and shortage of skilled workers. It was also a pilot project to determine the efficiency of varying low-cost building techniques for public housing.

Betondorp, which translates as "concrete village", was designed by a group of architects and construction companies to use 10 different concrete mixes. The layout roughly follows the self-contained communities of the garden-city movement, meaning the detached houses with private gardens are single-family dwellings centred around a communal square. Sitting next to this concrete cluster are an additional 1,000 homes built of brick and designed by architects Jan Gratama and Gerrit Versteeg.
Brink, 1097 TW

Old school
———
In an attempt to combat tuberculosis before the Second World War, the Dutch government commissioned *openlichtscholen* (open-air schools). The first was Eerste Openluchtschool, located on Cliostraat, designed by Jan Duiker and completed in 1930.

④
Krom Boomssloot
warehouses, Centrum
Lots in store

The double warehouses of Krom
Boomssloot were originally home
to naval workers and located
in an industrial shipping area.
Shipbuilder and former city mayor
Cornelis Pietersz Boom owned
them, hence the name.

Some of the façades, wooden
shutters and courtyards have been
preserved from the 17th century
and are now national monuments.
Highlights include the 1980s art
initiative Schottenburch (numbers
18 to 20) and the Armenian
Apostolic church (number 22)
but most are now apartments
with hefty price tags.
16-22 Krom Boomssloot, 1011 GW

5
Oostelijk Havengebied,
Eastern Docklands
Warehouse renovations

The docklands' 19th-century
warehouses were replaced
with high-density residential
developments between the late
1980s and early 2000s. Tour them
on two-wheels, starting at the
eastern peninsulas of Borneo and
Sporenburg, which feature three-
storey houses by urban designers
West 8. Three sculptural blocks
(look out for The Whale) stand
in stark contrast to these low-rise
waterfront dwellings.

Cycle along Stokerkade, looking
across the canal to the diverse
houses on Scheepstimmermanstraat,
which were designed by their
owners. Jo Coenen, known for
Amsterdam's public library,
designed KNSM-eiland, where
large blocks flank a grand avenue
overlooking the IJ. End further west
on the adjacent Java-eiland with
Sjoerd Soeters' contemporary take
on the historic Dutch canal house.
The Whale, 224 Baron GA, Tindalstraat

01

Between 1910 and 1930, the Amsterdam School movement dominated architecture in the city. However, architects who started out in the studio of Eduard Cuypers had been playing around with this style for a while: the exchange building, now called Beurs van Berlage, was finished in 1903, for example.

At the movement's core was the innovative use of cheap materials such as brick, wood and roof tiles. It valued the idea of integrating art disciplines through sculpture and intricate (and often curvaceous brick) details, as well as considered interiors.

The growing population and the housing shortage caused by destruction during the First World War also saw socialist, Catholic and Protestant housing corporations commission architects to build entire neighbourhoods such as Plan South and Plan West. Democratic and attractive, these were statements from the architects about beauty and art being accessible to all.

1 – 3 Olympic Stadium, Jan Wils, 1928
2 Olympisch Stadion, 1076 DE
4 – 5 De Dageraad, Michel de Klerk and Piet Kramer, 1919 to 1922
PL Takstraat, 1073 KK
6 – 7 Beurs Van Berlage, HP Berlage, 1903
243 Damrak, 1012 ZJ
8 – 10 Jeruzalemkerk, Ferdinand Jantzen, 1929
14 Jan Maijenstraat, 1056 SG
11 – 13 Vrijheidslaan, Michel de Klerk, 1921 to 1923
Vrijheidslaan, 1078 PJ

02 03

06

04

05 07

08

09

10

11

12

13

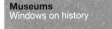

Museums
Windows on history

Museum Ons' Lieve Heer
op Solder, Centrum
Furtive votives

Religion in the Netherlands was
not openly tolerated in the 17th
century so discreet services had
to be held in homes. Many attics
concealed places of worship but
few have been preserved. Ons'
Lieve Heer op Solder (Our Lord in
the Attic) was built by a Catholic
merchant in 1663, spans four
buildings and is cut into the top
three storeys of canal houses.

Historians have tried to return
the church to its original design,
including the mauve of the walls
and balconies, discovered after
stripping back layers of paint.
While the audio tour, mandatory
booties and reimagined living
quarters may seem gimmicky, the
paradoxical relationship between
the church's concealment and
opulence is striking.
38 Oudezijds Voorburgwal,
1012 GE
+31 (0)20 624 6604
opsolder.nl

②
Architectuurcentrum Amsterdam,
Eastern Docklands
Building on the past

The curving Architectuurcentrum
Amsterdam (Arcam) building
was designed by Renzo Piano
and constructed as a pavilion for
the Nemo Science Museum (*see
page 116*) in 1997. When the site
was assigned to exhibitions on
architecture, urban-planning and
landscape design in 2003, Dutch
architect René van Zuuk was
enlisted to remodel it.

The existing floor and its
triangular shape with five columns
beneath were maintained. A wave-
like case of zinc-coated aluminium
was folded over the structure, while
a wall of glass provided views of the
docks. Two of the three storeys now
house simple exhibitions on the
city's design but catch the Crash
Course on Friday afternoons, when
staff run through nearly seven
centuries of architectural history.
600 Prins Hendrikkade, 1011 VX
+31 (0)20 620 4878
arcam.nl/en

Please don't break,
please don't break

③
Stadsarchief Amsterdam
De Bazel, Centrum
Records rooms

Karel de Bazel designed this
towering (by Amsterdam standards)
chequered stone building in 1926 for
the Dutch Trading Company. He
wanted his design to outlast fickle
trends rather than conform to any set
style. Sadly the building's subsequent
residents (which included a bank)
altered his vision, inserting partitions
and lowering ceilings.

In 2005 restoration architect
Maartin Fritz was enlisted to
reinstate de Bazel's intended
timelessness and create a home
for the city's archives. It opened as
Stadsarchief Amsterdam in 2007 and
holds extensive historical records on
the top four floors (the most valued
records are in the old basement
bank vaults). There is also a free
exhibition space that gives you a
good idea of the building's design.
*32 Vijzelstraat, 1017 HL.
+ 31 (0)20 251 1511
debazelamsterdam.nl;
archief.amsterdam*

④
Nemo Science Museum,
Eastern Docklands
Find it

Nemo's copper-green hull,
emerging from Oosterdok, is
one of the boldest designs on the
cityscape. Italian architect Renzo
Piano called Amsterdam "a one-
dimensional city" and this fuelled
his vision to create an elevated
piazza and observation terrace
on the building's roof.

Piano's main challenge was
using the IJtunnel as Nemo's
foundation. The tunnel inspired
his curved design: as it descends
below the river the museum
mirrors it, rising 22 metres above
the water. Since its completion
in 1997, Piano's design has
housed the Netherlands' leading
children's science and technology
museum. Its interior focuses
attention on exhibits by having
minimal windows, straightforward
orientation and neutral grey walls.
2 Oosterdok, 1011 VX
+31 (0)20 531 3233
nemosciencemuseum.nl/en

⑤
Museum Het Schip, Westerpark
Vessel for knowledge

Museum Het Schip is perhaps
the most iconic example of the
Amsterdam School style, designed
by Michel de Klerk and built
between 1917 and 1921 (Eduard
Cuypers discovered De Klerk at
the age of 14 and took him on as
a pencil sharpener).

Shaped roughly like a ship,
the building has played host to
a post office, primary school
and residential block. De Klerk
finished every detail with great
care, believing that giving people
somewhere beautiful to live would
encourage them to climb the social
and economic ladder. The building
still has about 80 social-housing
apartments but a large portion
is now open to the public as a
museum. To learn more about the
movement, its techniques and the
building, arrive for the museum's
15.00 tour in English.
45 Oostzaanstraat, 1013 WG
+31 (0)20 686 8595
hetschip.nl

Contemporary
Modern artistry

①
Cuyperspassage, Centrum
Underground movement

Beneath Centraal station is the
Cuyperspassage pedestrian-and-
cyclist tunnel that connects the
city with the ferries to the north
and services 15,000 commuters a
day. The 110-metre-long corridor
opened in 2015 and was designed
by Benthem Crouwel Architects
– who also designed Rai Car Park
(*see opposite*) – and graphic-design
luminary Irma Boom.

Before entering, stand on the
line that separates pedestrians from
cyclists; the contrasting colours and
lighting make the tunnel appear to
split in two. The walkway is covered
in 80,000 Delftware tiles, 46,000 of
which depict Boom's design of the
warship *Rotterdam* and the Herring
Fleet. By contrast, the cycle path is
unmarked asphalt and metal grates.
Centraal station, Stationsplein, 1012 AB

Changing skyline

Gaining approval for
development projects
within the city centre is near
impossible because most
buildings are under Unesco
World Heritage protection.
As such, city-planners and
developers are looking
to construct commercial,
residential and public buildings
in the outlying suburbs. Here
are a few projects to keep an
eye out for.

01 Bridge to Noord, Eastern
Docklands: The prospect
of a bridge that crosses
the IJ has been town-
planning fodder since
the early 1900s. But
more concrete plans
are forming for a joint
pedestrian-and-cyclists
bridge stretching
between Java-eiland and Noord.
02 Sluisbuurt,
Zeeburgereiland: This
highly controversial plan
is for a new high-rise
neighbourhood on an
industrial island in the
IJ harbour. Residential
towers will stand at about
130 metres tall, blocking
the view of residents in
the Noord.
03 Houthavens: Construction
for this climate-neutral
neighbourhood on a
decommissioned industrial
port in the west began
in 2010. A school and its
gym are already open and
the entire project, which
will include new islands for
housing blocks, is slated
for completion in 2021.

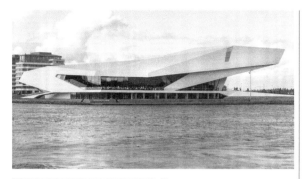

③
Rai Car Park, Zuidas
Ramped-up genius

Another noteworthy project from Benthem Crouwel Architects is the Rai Amsterdam Exhibition and Convention Centre carpark. The design of these two helix-shaped ramps draws comparison with the brutalist Marnixstraat Europarking complex but the co-founder, Mels Crouwel, says it came from the iconic principle of spiralling ramps. "We aimed to make it more fine and elegant," he says.

One downside if you're on foot: with a busy motorway beside it and only a narrow footpath, you may struggle to find yourself a good viewpoint.
Europaboulevard, 1078 RV

②
Eye Filmmuseum, Noord
Moving imagery

This landmark on the IJ riverfront was designed by Viennese studio Delugan Meissl, a catalyst for the regeneration of the neglected Noord. Completed in 2012 it's almost sculptural, with a dynamic shape that looks different from every angle.

The architects began with the notion that film and architecture share fundamentals such as the interplay of movement, light and space. The exterior flows into an open and bright interior with the foyer at its heart; whichever part of the building you visit, you always return to this central space.
1 IJpromenade, 1031 KT
+ 31 (0)20 589 1400
eyefilm.nl

Bridges

Amsterdam has about 1,200 bridges, from 17th-century drawbridges to postmodern, minimalist crossings. Here are some favourites.

01 Na-Druk-Geluk-Brug, Oud-Zuid: Designed by René van Zuuk Architekten in 2013 as part of a wider regeneration in Amsterdam Zuid. Minimal detailing and stark white deliberately contrast with Jan Wils' 1928 Olympic Stadium and the industrial blocks to the south.

02 Jan Schaeferbrug, Eastern Docklands: Ton Venhoeven's bridge spans 200 metres and links the eastern Java-eiland with the city. Every five years, two entire sections weighing about 200 tonnes are removed by barge to allow the tall ships of Sail Amsterdam to pass.

03 Borneo-Sporenburg, Eastern Docklands: Two red walkways connect the Borneo and Sporenburg residential islands in the Eastern Docklands. Completed in 2000 by West 8, the higher bridge has impressive views of the marina and allows boats to pass while the lower, more accessible one mirrors it at the opposite end of the harbour.

04 Magere Brug, Centrum: The original Skinny Bridge dates back to 1691; the current, wider drawbridge is from 1931. It's thought to have been commissioned by two sisters who lived on opposite sides of the canal but no one knows whether "skinny" refers to their surname, physique or penny-pinching budget.

❶
Gable stones, Jordaan
Addressing an issue

Houses weren't numbered in
Amsterdam until the late 19th
century so *gevelstenen* (gable
stones) were put above doorways
to differentiate properties. Peaking
in popularity in the 16th century,
they were normally decorated
with symbols of the inhabitant's
profession or family sign, or
occasionally an image from folklore.

The city has about 850 such
stone artworks including some
newer examples, mostly in Jordaan.
Look out for the two men and a
dog on Karthuizersstraat, which is
based on the fable of Amsterdam's
first settlers; the writing hand on
Egelantierstraat shows what was
once home to a schoolmaster.

②
De Gooyer windmill,
Eastern Docklands
Grind house

Windmills are synonymous with
the Netherlands and this octagonal
former corn mill, called De Gooyer,
was built in the 18th century. Its
wooden frame moved between
different locations until settling in
its current spot in 1814.

Although the interior is closed
to the public, you can still get up
close thanks to the pub next door.
Microbrewery Brouwerij 't IJ
was founded by musician Kaspar
Peterson in 1985 in the former
bathhouse next to the mill. Stop
by for a glass of organic beer and
sit on the terrace to enjoy the view
of De Gooyer.
5 Funenkade, 1018 AL

It's not quite the highest I've been in Amsterdam but it's close

Amsterdamse Krulletter
Font of originality

The curling, gregarious swirls of the traditional Amsterdamse Krulletter were fathered by Jan Willem Joseph Visser. It first started to appear in the 1940s on the windows of the city's *bruine* cafés and was funded by Heineken as a form of advertising. Visser was inspired by the late cancellaresca style, which calligraphers practised during the Dutch Golden Age.

"The letters that Visser created bear the distinctive features of the Baroque quill," says Ramiro Espinoza, Argentinian type designer and author of De Amsterdamse Krulletter (*see page 84*). "They've resisted the test of time and have been appropriated by Amsterdam's citizens as a true expression of their culture."

Bars across the city bear Visser's signage, from the oldest tavern Café Karpershoek to the wood-panelled Café Hegeraad.

④
Police branding
Eye-catching by law

Rolled out more than two decades ago, the branding of the Dutch emergency services is iconic. The orange, blue and white 45-degree stripes started out on police cars and bikes but more recently the fire, ambulance and rescue services have adopted them.

"Our design hasn't aged despite changes in car models and technology," says Liza Enebeis, creative director at Studio Dumbar, the agency behind the look. "Our stripes can even be found on speed cameras and drones." They're so popular that a special task force has been set up to prevent members of the public illegally sticking stripes onto their own cars.

⑤
City crest
Cross purposes

Contrary to the implications from gimmicky tourist trinkets, Amsterdam's city crest of xxx is not in any way related to the capital's tolerant stance towards vices. Instead the symbolism falls on the opposite end of the spectrum, representing Saint Andrew's cross.

Why the city employed the emblem of a 1st-century apostle crucified on an X-shaped cross is unknown. However, a pair of pliers sporting the three letters were recently discovered during the construction of the metro line and have been dated to 1350, suggesting that xxx is one of the oldest known examples of city branding.

Sport and fitness
—— Active city

Warmer months
Hot in the city

The people of Amsterdam aren't averse to exercise – how could they be in a city that's as renowned for its bicycle culture as it is for its canals? These waterways play a key part in the outdoor culture, whether it's cycling along them or simply enjoying the passing scenery from a boat as you float peacefully down them. During the colder months, when the water sometimes freezes, you're likely to spot the locals lacing up their skates and zipping across the ice (if the weather fails to co-operate you can still participate at a range of artificial rinks).

If you prefer your exercise to be a little more traditional there are also gyms (some more punishing than others), pools and tennis courts where you can get your heart rate up, or failing that check out our recommendations for a scenic run or two. And when you're done, refresh and revive at our selection of grooming hotspots and spa destinations. You'll have earned it.

①
Boat hire, citywide
Drift away

During the warmer months, rent a boat, pack a picnic and float towards the harbour or Amstel River. No licence is required for rentals, just a sober captain over 18 who can handle the intersections.

Mokum Boats rental locations include Centrum, Amstel and Oost. For a snack, dock along the quays at Café Hesp, Hannekes Boom or Waterkant. Or for a swim, head south for the widened section of the Amstel in front of the tHuis aan de Amstel café.
*Mokum Boats: Centrum, 351
Nassaukade, 1053 LZ; Amstel,
1 Schollenbrugstraat, 1091 EX;
Oost, 65 Mauritskade, 1092 AD
mokumbootverhuur.nl*

❷
Flevopark, Indische Buurt
Activity centre

Flevopark is wedged between the Indische Buurt neighbourhood and Nieuwe Diep Lake. Dutch conservationist and botanist Jac P Thijsse led the charge to develop the park to service the city's growing population; it was completed in 1931 for the Jewish community, then bought by the city in 1956 and opened to the public.

Today it's favoured by runners and in warm weather the outdoor pool opens and the lake is perfect for watersports. Barbecues are permitted in designated areas and the former watermill now houses a distillery and tasting room.
*Kramatweg, 1095 KD
flevopark.nl; nwediep.nl*

Amsterdam
Sport and fitness

Colder months
Just chill

Year-round
Perennial favourites

①
Ice-skating, citywide
Blade runners

As soon as the layer of ice on top of ditches, canals and lakes is firm, Amsterdammers get their skates on. Not every winter is cold enough nowadays, so from November to February there's an artificial rink in front of the Rijksmuseum, with skate rental and a café serving hot chocolate and glühwein.

Jaap Edenbaan in the east has a 400-metre loop open in the winter and an indoor rink all year round. During sub-zero temperatures, Amsterdamse Bosbaan in the south is the place to skate.
Rijksmuseum: 5 Museumplein, 1071 DJ; iceamsterdam.nl
Jaap Edenbaan: 64 Radioweg, 1098 NJ; jaapeden.nl

Sporting events

01 **Dam tot Damloop:**
This annual 16km road race sees 50,000 participants run from Amsterdam through the IJtunnel and the Dutch countryside to Zaandam.
damloop.nl

02 **Sail Amsterdam:**
Every five years more than 600 sailing ships from across the globe drop anchor in the IJ. Festivities take place both ashore and onboard the ships.
sail.nl

03 **Amsterdam Marathon:**
With 16,500 runners, the annual Amsterdam Marathon tours the Eastern Docklands, Zuid, Oud-West and a pretty stretch of the Amstel River.
tcsamsterdammarathon.nl

04 **Amsterdam City Swim:**
More than 2,000 swimmers dive into the canals in September to swim 2,000 metres, raising funds for Amyotrophic lateral sclerosis. Even Queen Máxima has taken part.
amsterdamcityswim.nl

High Studios, De Plantage
Gonna make you sweat

If the thought of a 45-minute fitness class doesn't seem all that daunting, think again. High Studios is tough: whole-body tough, enough to make you want to tell the very nice and encouraging instructor to kindly go away.

Barbara den Bak opened this sleek studio in 2016 and bases all of her classes on the principles of high-intensity interval training. Class sizes are small, single passes are available and we can guarantee you'll feel fantastic post-workout. You might just have to wait for the waves of nausea to subside first.
101 Weesperstraat, 1018 VN
+31 (0)20 890 3158
highstudios.com

I don't know what you're talking about, this is light as a feather

②
Tennisclub IJburg, IJburg
Hi, court

This club is a 30-minute cycle ride
(by Amsterdam standards it may as
well be halfway to Germany) but
if you fancy a game while in town,
the MVRDV-designed Tennisclub in
IJburg is worth the pedal.

The ruby-red clubhouse with
a café and changing rooms looks
out over pristine waters and its
roof doubles as a grandstand for
the 10 clay courts. This public
sporting complex was developed to
encourage Amsterdammers out to
the far-eastern neighbourhood, so
visitors don't need a membership
and it's open whatever the season.
1 Zandzeggestraat, 1087 SL
+31 (0)20 778 1671
tennisverenigingijburg.nl

③
Zuiderbad, Oud-Zuid
Decorative pool

The art deco Zuiderbad, which
abuts the Rijksmuseum, was
designed as an indoor driving
school by Jonas Ingenohl in 1897. It
didn't last long and soon became
a showroom, then in 1912 opened
as a swimming pool. Progressive
for its time, it had electric lighting,
central-heating and a sand-based
water-filtration system in the
basement, all of which still function.

While not the best spot for
serious swimmers, its mosaic tiling
and brass fixtures make a dramatic
setting for a few relaxing laps.
26 Hobbemastraat, 1071 ZC
+31 (0)20 252 1390
amsterdam.nl/zuiderbad

④
Akasha, Oud-Zuid
Underground club

One level below the glass atrium
of the Conservatorium Hotel is the
Amsterdam outpost for Akasha.
For short-term visitors, day passes
and monthly membership are
available. These afford access to
pilates, boxing and yoga classes, the
moderately sized but well-equipped
gym and the underground spa with
its pool, sauna and hamam.

The real treat is in the details,
from the smartly designed lockers
with retractable coat hangers to
the Netflix-enabled screens on
the treadmills.
Conservatorium Hotel, 27 Van
Baerlestraat, 1071 AN
+31 (0)20 570 0000
conservatoriumhotel.com

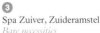

Grooming
Looking good

①

Wild Romance, Centrum
Pride and grooming

There's no shortage of good hairdressers in the Dutch capital but for the hat-trick of skilled staff, good music and strong coffee, you should consider a passionate fling with Wild Romance.

A host of seasoned freelancers operate out of the duplex studio, cutting, colouring and styling. A pretty little atrium with basins can be found up top, while a vintage-inspired barber is set up on the lower level. There's also a solid stack of the latest publications on hand including – ahem – one called Monocle. Make your booking online or in person.
62 Spuistraat, 1012 TW
wildromance.net

The Barber, Jordaan
Direct male

Avail yourself of a trim and a haircut the classic way in this smart barber's hidden on a cross street of trendy Haarlemmerdijk. A full menu of treatments covers everything from the traditional hot-towel and straight-razor shave to The Connery, the shop's amusingly monickered head shave for the follically challenged.

As well as offering its own range of beard products, aftershaves and oils, The Barber carries a selection from the likes of Hudson Made, Mr Natty and OAK. Oh, and coffee, beer or whiskey is on the house.
24 Binnen Oranjestraat, 1013 JA
+31 (0)20 337 3755
barber.nl

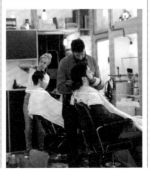

③

Spa Zuiver, Zuideramstel
Bare necessities

To work out the niggles of a long flight or just a long day, head south to Spa Zuiver on the border of the Amsterdamse Bos nature reserve. There's a seemingly endless array of pools, tubs and saunas to dip in and out of, including the outdoor spa and 40-metre lap pool surrounded by forest.

Fellow bathers tend to be nude but if you're not keen on that idea, swimwear is permitted on Tuesdays and Thursdays. There are also squash and tennis courts, as well as a catering service and 31 hotel rooms.
8 Koenenkade, 1081 KH
+31 (0)20 301 0700
zuiveramsterdam.nl

Football: Ajax

For those who concern themselves with such things, Dutch football has a mystical allure – and no team better represents this enchantment than Ajax (*see page 77*). The club's legend was sealed in the 1970s when, with Johan Cruyff, they won the European Cup three seasons in a row.

If you want to go and watch the latest incarnation of this fabled team, tickets can be bought online and collected at the ground (which can be reached by metro or bus). And if your visit doesn't coincide with a match day, you can take a guided tour instead.
ajax.nl

Whoops, see you later! Just call me Johan Wooyff

① Noord cycle tour
Waterways and green fields

The city centre isn't always the most relaxing place to wheel around so try the north's rural paths instead.

STARTING POINT: Centraal station, Centrum
DISTANCE: 10km

Rent your *fiets* (bicycle) from MacBike, around the back of Centraal station. Take the 902 ferry to ❶ *IJplein*, drinking in the views over the city, and once docked pedal northeast along Meeuwenlaan. Cross the first roundabout and just after the road forks take a sharp right onto pretty Nieuwendammerdijk (*see page 109*), a quaint street with charming old houses.

Take a break in ❷ *Café 't Sluisje*, a historic *bruin* café in a building that's nearly 500 years old and has a large waterside terrace that's perfect for lunch. Continue straight along the same road, passing fields and waterways as you go, until it ends at a park.

Turn right over the white bridge, immediately left and then keep right on Schellingwouderdijk. After you've passed some football pitches, turn right down Noorder IJdijk and dismount when you reach the start of the ❸ *Oranjesluizen*. To cross this series of working locks you'll have to go by foot.

Once you're back on your bike head down Zuider IJdijk, joining the two upper paths nearest the water. At the T-junction turn right and follow the path to a big bridge; wheel your bike up the tracks on the nearside stairway. Head west along Zuiderzeeweg until the junction, where you turn right onto Zeeburgerdijk. Continue for 1.5km until you see the De Gooyer windmill (*see page 120*) over the water to your right. Once you reach it, it would be impolite not to reward yourself with a beer at adjacent brewery ❹ *Brouwerij 't IJ*.

① Vondelpark
Park run

DISTANCE: 4.3km
GRADIENT: Flat
DIFFICULTY: Easy
HIGHLIGHT: The stretch along the southern pond
BEST TIME: Take your pick
NEAREST STATION: Rijksmuseum

Start at the main entrance of the park on *Stadhouderskade* and head west under the bridge designed by Piet Kramer in 1947. Next you'll enter the main park; take the first right to follow the road that loops around the pond. Look out for the neo-gothic *Vondelkerk* on the right, designed by Pierre Cuypers, the man behind the Rijksmuseum (*see page 91*). At the fork in the path, leave the main road and head right on the narrow path that meanders along the edge of the park, passing Roman church-turned-music-venue *Orgelpark*.

As you rejoin the main road, take a sharp right and carry on for about 700 metres. At the end follow the curve to your left and once you've crossed the water (marked by knee-high walls) take a right to run along the narrow path. Rejoin the main road and after about 300 metres take the lakeside path again.

At the next fork, keep left and then head back onto the main road. Veer right, passing "Figure Découpée (L'Oiseau)" in the clearing on your left. This sculpture was designed by Picasso and presented to the city in 1965. Loop right around the pond and on the left look for a blue bridge to the *Blauwe Theehuis* (Blue Teahouse), a modernist institution built in the 1930s. Finish here with a drink or loop around the building and continue on to pass the statue of Dutch poet Joost van den Vondel, after whom the park was named. You'll wind up back at the starting point.

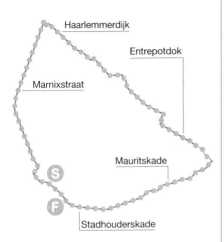

(2)
Outer canal ring
Round trip

DISTANCE: 10km
GRADIENT: Flat
DIFFICULTY: Moderate
HIGHLIGHT: The changing architecture
BEST TIME: Early morning to beat the traffic
NEAREST STATION: Rijksmuseum

Start anywhere on the outer canal ring, depending on where you're staying; we'll start across from the *Rijksmuseum*, going anti-clockwise around Centrum. Avoid the red bike path and stick to the footpath, which sporadically becomes a carpark over the next kilometre. Cross at Weteringlaan and head along the canal past the old *Heineken Brewery*. Cross Westeinde, with De Nederlandsche Bank on your left.

The road inclines to cross the Amstel. Bear right at the Wibautstraat intersection, following the pedestrian crossings. At the statue of *Dr FM Wibaut* run east along the canal to the Olifantsbrug. Cross it, head down the passage through the building ahead, then cross Sarphatistraat and take the wooden bridge to run past the new blocks on Entrepotdok. Follow the road almost to the end, veer right down another passage, then left over the green drawbridge.

Turn right towards Arcam (*see page 114*), then left along Prins Hendrikkade. Pass by *Grand Hotel Amrâth* (*see page 25*) then as you pass Hotel NH Collection, veer right to cross the canal. At the next canal turn left then right along Haarlemmerstraat, which turns into Haarlemmerdijk retail strip. Cross the square, approach the concrete Haarlemmerpoort arcade and turn left on Korte Marnixstraat. This final leg is inside the canal ring, an uninterrupted stretch of footpath. At the Apple store head right over the canal and then left to finish by the Rijksmuseum.

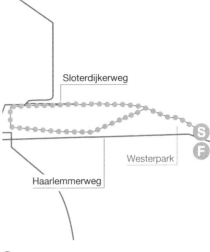

(3)
Westerpark
Canal tour

DISTANCE: 5km
GRADIENT: Flat
DIFFICULTY: Moderate
HIGHLIGHT: Scenic views of canals (and a windmill)
BEST TIME: Mornings if you're a dog-lover
NEAREST STATION: Haarlemmerplein

It's easy to clock some kilometres in Westerpark. The manicured garden dotted with sculptures joins the old gasworks, now restaurants and bars, and tracks extend north and west through the less-maintained greenery.

Start at the Westerpark entrance (at the junction of *Houtmankade* and *Westerpark*), following the main footpath northwest; at the tennis courts follow the paved path as it veers slightly right. You'll soon be running in line with the train and when the path ends cross the thoroughfare (look out for cyclists) and continue along the footpath opposite.

The next leg is a simple loop around the western residential stretch of the parklands, along a gravel path with wild foliage on either side. At the carpark look for the path on your left and follow it down the gentle slope to the end. Continue adjacent to *Sloterdijkerweg* for about 200 metres then follow the path as it turns left to re-enter the parklands. Go left again at the next corner and run along the tree-lined footpath, bordered by the residential plots on your left and a commercial complex on your right.

As you approach the cylindrical building of the *Westergasfabriek* (Western Gasworks) you'll reach a junction. If you're feeling fit take a left towards and under the train line for a short lap around a city farm; if you're ready to wind down head straight back towards Westerpark. At the train line follow the path on which you entered the park.

127

Walks
—— Best foot forward

It is no secret that the bicycle is considered king in Amsterdam but unfortunately that is to the detriment of pedestrians. Footpaths are often narrow, sometimes blocked and occasionally disappear altogether without warning. However, it's worth persevering because the compact nature of neighbourhoods is perfect for exploring food, retail and culture offerings on foot – just make sure you mind your step in the process.

NEIGHBOURHOOD 01

Oost
On the up

To experience the less-polished side of Amsterdam, head to the city's energetic east. Here you'll find the fruits of the Netherlands' prolific colonial exploits, particularly in the names of the streets. Once considered a part of town best avoided, today things are on the rise as students and artists arrive in search of cheaper rent and the neighbourhood becomes more diverse.

The walk begins in an area known as Oud-Oost (Old East), which is not as old as its name might suggest: it only dates back to the late 19th century and was built to give labourers more affordable housing – the Dubbeltjespanden is a particularly charming example. The area's green lung is Oosterpark, packed with interesting sculptures and inviting reading spots, and on its outskirts are several notable historical sights, including the country's biggest wooden windmill. The second half of the walk takes in the century-old Indische Buurt, named after the Dutch East Indies (present-day Indonesia). Its beating heart is Javastraat, a vibrant mix of ethnic food shops, boutiques, trendy bars and great restaurants.

Often compared to New York's Brooklyn, Oost is where the tidy picture-perfect canals of central Amsterdam give way to the grittier hustle and bustle of a truly diverse neighbourhood.

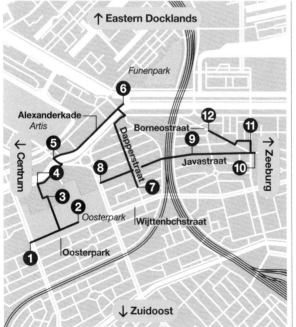

Lively spirit
Oost walk

Start off with a coffee and a bite to eat at ❶ *Bar Bukowski* then walk round the left-hand side of Oosterpark to find the nearest entrance. When it opened in 1891, Oosterpark was the first major public green space in the city (Vondelpark is older but was initially private). These days it's home to dozens of works of art such as ❷ *De Schreeuw*, a tribute to film-maker Theo van Gogh who

was murdered in 2004 after he made a controversial film about women in Islam. The stainless-steel work is between the park's two southeastern entrances.

Leave the park heading north, keeping the Generator Hostel on your left, and join Mauritskade. Just before you hit the main road, check out ❸ *VanMoof*, an award-winning specialist bike shop that also offers free worldwide shipping. From there turn left and then immediately left again into quaint ❹ *Dubbeltjespanden* (literally, "dime buildings", named after the original weekly rental cost). This was one of the first examples of social housing in the Netherlands when construction began in 1870. The brick shelves with white silhouettes of objects tell the stories of the street's residents over the decades.

Before leaving make sure you look across the water: that feast of brick and glass is a former medicine-storage building. It was reimagined by US architect Steven Holl and is now part of a housing association.

Walk east towards the imposing Tropenmuseum (*see page 139*), which is worth a visit if you have a spare hour or two. Otherwise cross the bridge in front of it and admire the grand ❺ *Muiderpoort* archway, the only remaining gate from Amsterdam's old fortifications. It was built in the Louis XVI style in the 18th century and Napoleon rode through it in 1811 after conquering the city.

Return to the Singelgracht and walk along Alexanderkade until you reach the delightful De Gooyer windmill. The tallest in the country, it is now a private home but you

can enjoy a good view of the exterior along with a beer and some *bitterballen* (deep-fried snacks) at the neighbouring brewery, ❻ *Brouwerij 't IJ* (*see page 120*).

Cross the bridge and rejoin Mauritskade before diving into one of Oost's gems: the raucous ❼ *Dappermarkt*. With stalls selling everything from Arabic rugs to fish, this is where the neighbourhood meets, mingles and shops. Take your time and amble down to Eerste van Swindenstraat and then turn left. Continue walking until you see ❽ *Roopram Roti* just before the end of the road. This place won't win any awards for decor but, as the queues suggest, it's second-to-none for Surinamese food. Try the lamb or *pom* (chicken) roti for a cheap and cheerful lunch.

Double back on yourself and continue straight ahead under the train bridge. This is the beginning of Javastraat, the perfect place to find one-off clothes and hard-to-find spices. There's an afternoon's worth of exploring to be done here but don't miss ❾ *The Other Guys* for edgy local and international fashion brands.

At the end of the street grab a burger or some freshly grilled fish at the unmissable ❿ *Het Badhuis*, a well-preserved former bathhouse that was still in use well into the second half of the 20th century.

To continue your evening, head north up Molukkenstraat to ⓫ *Bar Joost* to enjoy some more Dutch beer. Or follow Borneostraat and catch a film at ⓬ *Studio K*, a quirky student-run association that also hosts club nights and cultural events.

Address book

01 Bar Bukowski
10 Oosterpark, 1092 AE
+31 (0)20 370 1685
barbukowski.nl

02 De Schreeuw
Oosterpark, 1092 AS

03 VanMoof
55 Mauritskade, 1092 AD
+31 (0)20 330 7401
vanmoof.com

04 Dubbeltjespanden
29-54 Mauritskade,
1092 AA
dubbeltjespanden.nl

05 Muiderpoort
500 Sarphatistraat,
1018 AV

06 Brouwerij 't IJ
7 Funenkade, 1018 AZ
+31 (0)20 528 6237
brouwerijhetij.nl

07 Dappermarkt
Dapperstraat, 1093 BS
+31 (0)20 694 7495
dappermarkt.nl

08 Roopram Roti
4 Eerste van
Swindenstraat, 1093 GC
+31 (0)20 693 2902
roopramroti.nl

09 The Other Guys
51 Javastraat, 1094 HA
+31 (0)20 233 7825

10 Het Badhuis
21 Javaplein, 1095 CJ
+31 (0)20 665 1226

11 Bar Joost
33 Molukkenstraat,
1095 AT
+31 (0)62 903 6092
joost-amsterdam.nl

12 Studio K
62 Timorplein, 1094 CC
+31 (0)20 692 0422
studio-k.nu

Getting there

Trams 3 and 7 cross the entire city and stop at Beukenweg station next to Bar Bukowski. Metro lines 51, 53 and 54 start at Centraal station and stop at Wibautstraat, five minutes from the starting point. It is also a 10-minute cycle from the centre.

NEIGHBOURHOOD 02
Oud-West
Creatively inclined

Centuries ago this neighbourhood was little more than farmland, home to a smattering of country residences belonging to the rich and the location for some of Amsterdam's less-salubrious establishments, such as tanneries and a plague house. It wasn't until the late 19th century that construction began in earnest to make room for working-class families, meaning that, like Oud-Oost, Oud-West is not as old as you might think.

The area has been gentrified over the past decade, introducing new shops, cafés, bars and restaurants beloved by the city's creative residents. While it lacks museums and other traditional tourist attractions there are plenty of examples of clever rejuvenation, from a former tram depot to an old pathology laboratory, as well as an array of Amsterdam School buildings. Home to nearly 180 different nationalities, the neighbourhood's diversity is evident in its proximity to Westermoskee – the largest mosque in the Netherlands – and the bustling Ten Kate Market. At the same time, the area continues to feel traditionally Dutch and many of the streets are named after notable national poets, including Johannes Kinker (look out for the plaques).

This walk will lead you through this compact and casual area and invite you to follow in the footsteps of its residents.

Architecture and art
Oud-West walk

Start in Kwakersplein, a square that was once a lake surrounded by windmills. Keep an eye out for ❶ *De Ratelaar*, a bronze statue that honours the city's rubbish-collectors. The sound of their rattles calling for people to bring their rubbish out was once a key part of Amsterdam's soundscape. Behind the sculpture is ❷ *Berry*, where you can grab a coffee and a muffin.

Cross the canal and turn left onto the tiny Tollensstraat to reach the ❸ *De Hallen* complex. A former tram depot, it now houses a cinema, indoor food market, hairdresser, dance studio and several independent shops selling everything from olive oil and ceramics to jeans and photography. Enter the small building on your left first and walk through the larger building opposite. Exit onto the truly local ❹ *Ten Kate Market*, a great place for people-watching.

Head west along Bellamystraat, a historical street with a village

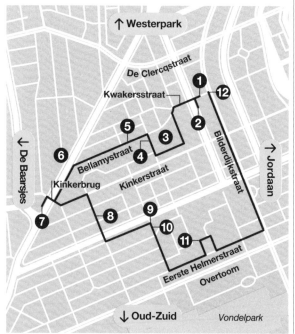

feel. The ❺ *Olympiagebouw* started out as a stable yard for a Dutch delivery company, then from the 1920s to the 1960s was a neighbourhood cinema known as the "flea pit". It later became a mosque and Turkish cultural centre and today it's a dance school.

Walk to Tweede Kostverlorenkade and pause to take in the massive ❻ *Westermoskee* across the water. The biggest mosque in the Netherlands, it was designed by French architects Marc and Nada Breitman, who used red brick and other features inspired by Amsterdam School and architect HP Berlage to make it blend in with its surroundings. It was – and still is – controversial and took 20 years to complete.

Walk left along the canal and cross the next bridge towards Het Sieraad. An excellent example of Amsterdam School architecture with its curving brick façade and embellishments, this iconic building started life in the 1920s as a trade school. The adjoining **7** *Lokaal Edel* is the perfect place to enjoy a cold beer and some lunch on the large canal-side terrace.

Appetite sated, cross back over the same bridge and take the second right off Kinkerstraat and onto Jan Pieter Heijestraat, a hidden gem of a shopping street. **8** *Dépôt by Johnny at the Spot* has wonderfully unusual homeware and clothes, for example. Once you've finished pottering around the area, cross over Jacob van Lennepkanaal and immediately turn left. At the end of Jacob van Lennepkade you'll find a wall with several small **9** *Hildo Krop*

sculptures. Krop was arguably one of the most important Amsterdam School artists.

Behind the wall is a building that used to be the pathology and anatomy laboratory for nearby Wilhelmina Hospital. It has now been transformed into a creative hub with shared offices, a great café and an arthouse cinema. It's known as **10** *Lab 111*.

Walking south, turn onto Eerste Helmersstraat to find the grand entrance to the former hospital, a sprawling complex built on the site of the city's 17th-century plague house. Opened in 1893, the hospital was in action for 90 years before being converted into flats, artists' residences, a hostel and a café known as the **11** *WG-square*. Go through the archway and explore the site before returning to Eerste Constantijn Huygensstraat.

Turn left and continue walking for a few minutes until you get to **12** *Happyhappyjoyjoy*. With a large menu of Asian drinks and street food, this is the perfect place to end the walk and start your evening.

Getting there

Trams 3 and 12 stop at Kinkerstraat while trams 7 and 17 (from Centraal station) stop at Bilderdijk/ Kinkerstraat, both of which are a one-minute walk from the starting point. It is also a 10-minute cycle from the centre.

Address book

01 De Ratelaar
Kwakersplein, 1053 VH

02 Berry
27 Bilderdijkkade,
1053 VH
+31 (0)20 370 7300
berryamsterdam.nl

03 De Hallen
47 Hannie
Dankbaarpassage,
1053 RT
+31 (0)20 705 8164
dehallen-amsterdam.nl

04 Ten Kate Market
97-99 Ten Katestraat,
1053 CC
tenkatemarkt.nl

05 Olympiagebouw
49 Bellamystraat, 1053 BG

06 Westermoskee
101 Piri Reïsplein,
1057 KH
westermoskee.nl

07 Lokaal Edel
1 Postjesweg, 1057 DT
+31 (0)20 799 5000
edelamsterdam.nl

08 Dépôt by Johnny at
the Spot
90-94 Jan Pieter
Heijestraat, 1053 GS
+31 (0)20 489 3868
johnnyatthespot.com

09 Hildo Krop sculptures
305 Nicolaas Beetsstraat,
1054 NZ

10 Lab 111
111 Arie Biemondstraat,
1054 PD
+31 (0)20 616 9994
lab111.nl

11 WG-square
9 Helmersplantsoen,
1054 RZ

12 Happyhappyjoyjoy
158HS Bilderdijkstraat,
1083 LC
+31 (0)20 344 6433
happyhappyjoyjoy.asia

NEIGHBOURHOOD 03
Jordaan
Hot property

Jordaan is arguably one of the most well-known neighbourhoods not only in Amsterdam but in the Netherlands. Its decades-long path to gentrification has seen galleries, top restaurants and high-end independent retail transform the area.

The neighbourhood was initially built when the city centre and its network of canals was doubled in the early 17th century. The area was developed for both industry and the working classes, who would service those living in the prestigious canal ring nearby. Warehouses for breweries, paper mills and small-scale factories were built along the wider canals to allow access for cargo liners. While wandering, cast your eyes up at the gable stones hinting at what the buildings once housed.

Workers' homes were built narrow as property taxes were calculated on the width of the façades; by the 19th century the overcrowded area had become a slum. However, some wealthier families funded construction of residential blocks for the poor. *Hofjes*, as they were known, were built around a courtyard and adhered to a set of rules enforced by a regent. Rooms were diminutive but many have now been renovated to align with modern standards. Today, close-knit residents and an increasingly international community populate the quiet cobbled streets. It's easy to see why Jordaan is a desirable place to dwell.

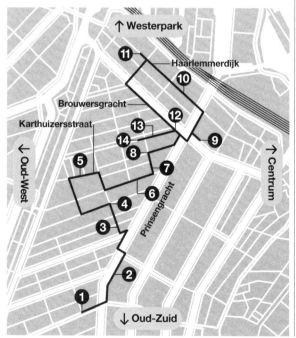

History lesson
Jordaan walk

Begin with a simple breakfast and a coffee at ❶ *Kessens*. Co-owner Casper Holtkamp's family runs the city's much-loved Patisserie Holtkamp and the pastries also feature on Kessens' menu. Exit and head east to cross the canal and take the first left passing Westerkerk to reach the ❷ *Anne Frank House*. Between 09.00 and 15.30 you can only enter if you've bought tickets in advance, so do book ahead. The

museum tells the poignant story of Anne Frank and the Netherlands during the Holocaust.

Exit the museum and walk north to Leliegracht, then cross the canal and turn right. Cross yet another bridge and head west, then take the first right and stop at ❸ *Back Beat Records* to pick up some soul, funk or jazz on vinyl. Walk north on Eerste Tuindwarsstraat for another couple of blocks to reach ❹ *Nils Kalf Schoenmaker* on the corner. Cobbler Nils Kalf has been making and repairing shoes for three decades.

Head north on Eerste Anjeliersdwarsstraat and continue onto Tweede Boomdwarsstraat, then turn left on Karthuizersstraat. At the entrance to houses 89 to 171 follow the stone tiles through to the inner courtyard of ❺ *Karthuizer Hofje*. This particular *hofje* (almshouse) opened in 1650 to house widows and their children and was the largest of its kind in the city. Exit back past the original clotheslines and head right to the end of the street, then right again and left onto the bustling strip of Westerstraat.

On the opposite side of the street is nostalgia-packed toyshop **⑥** *Mechanisch Speelgoed*. After exploring the floor-to-ceiling collection of toys, continue along Westerstraat until you pick up the scent of freshly baked apple pie. The petite **⑦** *Winkel 43* kitchen works tirelessly to keep up with demand and the lunch menu comes recommended if you're after something savoury.

Across the street is the protestant **⑧** *Noorderkerk*, dating from the 16th century. The church was painstakingly restored between 1989 and 2005 and hosts a classical concert every Saturday at 14.00 from September to June. Head east across the square and cross the canal twice, first at Lekkeresluis then at Papiermolensluis, and take note of the two dried fish above the entrance of **⑨** *162 Brouwersgracht*. From 1821 to 1971 the fish merchant Smit & Zoon operated from this warehouse.

Turn 180 degrees to snap a postcard-ready picture of the canal houses then walk north on Korte Prinsengracht and cross the bridge on your left before heading west on Haarlemmerdijk. An entire afternoon can be whiled away on this retail strip. We recommend taking a look around menswear and homeware shop **⑩** *Six and Sons* at number 31 and cookbook specialist **⑪** *De Kookboekhandel* at number 133.

After your retail fix, head back south via Binnen Dommersstraat, crossing the drawbridge to walk east along Brouwersgracht, named after the breweries that once populated the warehouses along this canal. With beer in mind, stop in for a lager or two at the homely corner spot **⑫** *Café Thijssen*, named after Jordaan resident and writer Theo Thijssen.

When hunger strikes, exit the bar and turn right, stopping outside **⑬** *55 Lindengracht* to look up at the humorous gable stone of a topsy-turvy world. Unlike the other centuries-old stones in the area, this one is from 1972 and nods to the fact that the street was a canal until 1895. Finish your walk with an Italian meal just a few doors down at **⑭** *Toscanini*.

Getting there

Trams 13, 14 and 17 servicing Oud-West, the centre and Eastern Docklands all stop at Westermarkt Station, which is a two-minute walk from the starting point. Alternatively, if you're on two wheels, Jordaan is a 10 to 15-minute pedal from most central locations.

Address book

01 Kessens
24 Rozengracht, 1016 NC
+31 (0)20 221 7431
kessensamsterdam.nl

02 Anne Frank House
263-267 Prinsengracht,
1016 GV
+31 (0)20 556 7105
annefrank.org

03 Back Beat Records
19 Egelantiersstraat,
1015 PV
+31 (0)20 627 1657
backbeat.nl

04 Nils Kalf Schoenmaker
2A Eerste Tuindwarsstraat,
1015 RV
+31 (0)20 623 4962
nilskalfschoenmaker.nl

05 Karthuizer Hofje
157 Karthuizersstraat,
1015 LP

06 Mechanisch Speelgoed
67 HS Westerstraat,
1015 LW
+31 (0)20 638 1680
mechanisch-speelgoed.nl

07 Winkel 43
43 Noordermarkt, 1015 NA
+31 (0)20 623 0223
winkel43.nl

08 Noorderkerk
44-48 Noordermarkt,
1015 NA
+31 (0)62 420 5631
noorderkerk.nl

09 162 Brouwersgracht
1013 HA

10 Six and Sons
31 Haarlemmerdijk, 1013 KA
+31 (0)20 233 0092
sixandsons.com

11 De Kookboekhandel
133 Haarlemmerdijk,
1013 KG
+31 (0)20 622 4768
kookboekhandel.com

12 Café Thijssen
107 Brouwersgracht,
1015 GD
+31 (0)20 623 8994
cafethijssen.nl

13 55 Lindengracht 1015 KC

14 Toscanini
75 Lindengracht, 1015 KD
+31 (0)20 623 2813
restauranttoscanini.nl

NEIGHBOURHOOD 04
Bos en Lommer and De Baarsjes
Back to school

Strolling on foot from Rembrandtpark through De Baarsjes and up to Erasmuspark in Bos en Lommer is a good way to take in Amsterdam School style (*see page 112*). As the city struggled to deal with a housing shortage after the First World War, swathes of farmland were redeveloped and architects were commissioned by housing corporations to design entire neighbourhoods. After designing Plan Zuid, modernist Dutch architect HP Berlage drafted Plan West, which lies within this neighbourhood.

A team of 16 Amsterdam School architects, including Johan van der Mey and Piet Kramer, helped design the grids of distinct brick apartment blocks. Two architects and the head of public works supervised each design to maintain cohesion. About 6,000 homes were built over a two-year period and Berlage himself designed Mercatorplein, the nucleus of community life.

These structures have since survived the Second World War and the demolition-happy councils of the late 20th century. Today the adjoining neighbourhoods continue to expand and the young, multicultural demographic is growing. It's true that Mercatorplein and Jan Evertsenstraat can still feel a little rough around the edges but the independent retailers and restaurants have started moving in.

School trip
*Bos en Lommer and
De Baarsjes walk*

Begin with a hearty breakfast at ❶ *Café DS*. Tucked away at the back of an industrial complex, this retro dining room (think palms, chequered floors and the odd pink wall) is part of entertainment venue De School (*see page 97*).

After some eggs and a quick peek around the complex, head out past the Reade medical centre, cross over the bridge and pass the Ramada Apollo hotel to enter ❷ *Rembrandtpark*. Named after the prolific Dutch painter Rembrandt Harmenszoon van Rijn, the park was opened in 1958 and has a petting zoo, outdoor gym and prime picnicking spots.

Follow the pedestrian path east to cross the lake or meander a little further south before exiting on Willem Schoutenstraat. Head east past the rows of Amsterdam School housing blocks and continue as the road gives way to a footpath. Turn left on Vasco Da Gamastraat, left again at the

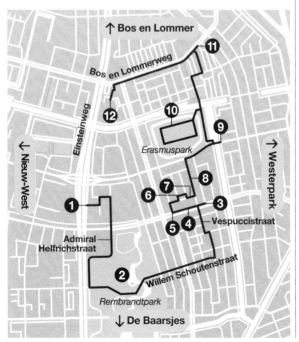

end of the street then hook a right onto Vespuccistraat past the newer residential builds.

When you emerge onto the high street of Jan Evertsenstraat, traverse the pedestrian crossing to your right and enter the verdant retailer ❸ *De Balkonie*. As the name suggests, this shop stocks all the mod cons you could ever wish for when decorating your balcony. Pick up some flower bulbs or a luggage-friendly pot then walk west and stop for a massage at ❹ *Het Massagehuys*.

With this in mind, bear north towards the park but before you enter take a right on Jan van Galenstraat to reach ❾ *Vier Windstrekenbrug*. Each corner of the bridge features a sculpture by Dutch artist Hildo Krop, representing the Earth's four cardinal points: there's an Inuit and seals for the north; a warrior and lions for the south; a Chinese man and trading ships for the east; and a man wearing a suit and holding a telephone for the west.

Once you've seen all four posts, take the stairs guarded by sculptor Jan Trapman's polar bear and tiger down to ❿ *Erasmuspark*. This park opened in 1939 and was named after the Dutch renaissance theologian Desiderius Erasmus. The flower garden on the opposite side of the canal bursts with colour during spring.

After a lap around the park return to the northern corner and cross the bridge to walk through Wachterliedplantsoen. Pass the playground and basketball court then turn right on Reinaert de Vosstraat and left on Merlijnstraat, continuing until you reach the stark white tiles of ⓫ *Podium Mozaïek*. This former church now acts as a cultural hub for the west. After catching a live show or simply admiring how the light streams into the building through the patterned tiles, walk west along Bos en Lommerweg.

Just after Hoofdweg, pass beneath the brick building and cut diagonally across the grass to finish with a wood-fired pizza and a craft beer at ⓬ *Wilde Westen*.

Getting there

Tram 13 and bus routes 302 and 752, all from Centraal station, stop just outside De School. Alternatively, tram 7 from the east stops just outside White Label Coffee and is a five-minute walk from the starting point.

Next stop is ❺ *White Label Coffee*. The brand has been roasting some of the city's best beans since 2013; we recommend one of the heady filter coffees. Continue west, then turn right at Aladdin's to walk beneath the clock tower and turn right again.

The street opens out onto a square with the boxy red-brick ❻ *Jeruzalemkerk* on the northern edge. Completed by Ferdinand Jantzen in 1929, the church was designed to fit in with the surrounding Amsterdam School architecture. Weather permitting, pull up a chair in the square and enjoy a *borrel* (drink) at ❼ *Café Cook*.

To continue your Amsterdam School appreciation tour, leave Café Cook and walk east on Jan Maijenstraat then turn left onto ❽ *Vespuccistraat*. When the leaves on the ginkgo biloba trees change colour in autumn, this is one of the most picturesque streets of the Plan West development. Completed by Jordanus Roodenburgh in 1926, the street was designed as a pretty pathway between Mercatorplein and Erasmuspark.

Address book

01 Café DS
1 Jan van Breemenstraat,
1056 AB
+31 (0)20 737 3197
deschoolamsterdam.nl

02 Rembrandtpark
Jan Evertsenstraat,
1056 AB

03 De Balkonie
90 Jan Evertsenstraat,
1056 EG
+31 (0)62 871 0318
debalkonie.nl

04 Het Massagehuys
110 Jan Evertsenstraat,
1056 EH
+31 (0)20 612 3251
massagehuys.nl

05 White Label Coffee
136 Jan Evertsenstraat,
1056 EK
+31 (0)20 737 1359
whitelabelcoffee.nl

06 Jeruzalemkerk
14 Jan Maijenstraat,
1056 SG
+31 (0)20 412 1452
jeruzalem-kerk.nl

07 Café Cook
2 James Cookstraat,
1056 RZ
+31 (0)20 612 0547
cafecook.nl

08 Vespuccistraat
Vespuccistraat, 1056 SH

09 Vier Windstrekenbrug
Jan van Galenstraat,
1056 BS

10 Erasmuspark
Jan van Galenstraat,
1056 BS

11 Podium Mozaïek
191 Bos en Lommerweg,
1055 DT
+31 (0)20 580 0380
podiummozaiek.nl

12 Wilde Westen
1 Bos en Lommerplantsoen,
1055 AA
+31 (0)20 760 8290
wilde-westen.nl

NEIGHBOURHOOD 05

De Pijp
Bohemian energy

The name "The Pipe" most likely refers to a narrow stretch of water that once cut through this neighbourhood. At the end of the 19th century the ditch was drained and replaced with the expansive market on Albert Cuypstraat. The market's diversity has permeated De Pijp's character and the high concentration of international cuisine, from Moroccan to Surinamese, is testament to the 140-plus nationalities that live and work here. Today the market itself may be a tourist trap but the wider neighbourhood has preserved its original bohemian energy.

Artists, students and writers moved in at the beginning of the 20th century, transforming the area into the city's Latin Quarter. Oude Pijp is still home to artists, who mark their studios with the sign: "Made in De Pijp". The neighbourhood's proximity to the northern canal district and its affordable (though rising) rent also appeal to creative entrepreneurs and independent-shop owners on Gerard Doustraat.

Nieuwe Pijp is more tranquil and residential. An early 20th-century Haussmann-style plan was never realised and instead made way for a social-democratic plan prioritising low-cost housing. This once-quiet area is slowly filling out with restaurants and bars and the highlight is the Dageraad, an architectural tour de force.

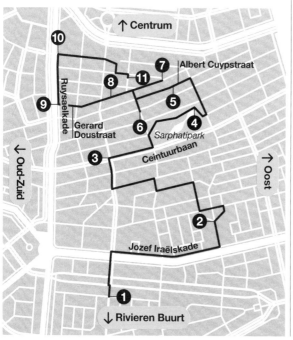

Market meander
De Pijp walk

Start with a *kopje koffie* (cup of coffee) and breakfast at ❶ *Vinnies* then head north towards Ferdinand Bolstraat and cross over the Amstelkanaal, passing the petite cone-shaped bridge houses designed by Amsterdam School architect Piet Kramer. Turn right to amble along the canal (the southern border of De Pijp) until you reach Pieter Lodewijk Takstraat. Pause on the corner, looking up at the integrated sculptures of Hildo Krop perched on the Berlage Lyceum. Here begins the Dageraad, which was commissioned by the eponymous housing association and completed in 1921. The visionary social-housing estate by Michel de Klerk and Piet Kramer contains 294 flats and became a monument for the labour movement.

As you walk up Pieter Lodewijk Takstraat admire the brickwork and uniform windows. At the junction look back at one of the flagship buildings of the movement, which

now houses the ❷ *Bezoekerscentrum De Dageraad*. This information centre operates under the Museum Het Schip (*see page 117*) and is dedicated to the Amsterdam School movement. Pop in to explore further or simply marvel at the decorative masonry on the façade.

Veer right along Burgemeester Tellegenstraat then turn left onto Coöperatiehof; at the end of the street, head north. Turn left at Karel du Jardinstraat, right through the Van der Helstplein and left again onto the Rustenburgerstraat. You

Getting there

The starting point is a 10-minute cycle from the canal ring. Alternatively, Scheldestraat Station is a block away and is serviced by tram 12 from the west, bus 65 from the Eastern Docklands and bus 246 that passes through Centrum.

will notice the change in architecture, indicating you are moving towards Oude Pijp.

When you hit the busy Ferdinand Bolstraat, turn right and at the Ceintuurbaan, right again. Stop for another coffee or a fresh ginger tea at ❸ *CT Coffee & Coconuts* and look up at the 1920s art deco façade of this former cinema complex. Once refuelled, head east.

When you pass Rialto cinema (arthouse enthusiasts take note) cross the street and continue, then turn right into Sarphatipark, named after Samuel Sarphati, physician and advocate for the wellbeing of the working classes. Walk northeast to the ❹ *Sarphati Viewpoint* on the bridge. Take in the views of the park designed in the English-garden style. Follow the footpath southeast to the exit then turn left and left again to stroll among the cheese and tulip stalls along Albert Cuypstraat. If you're hungry, grab a *stroopwafel* from ❺ *Original Stroopwafels* market stall or a pickled-herring sandwich at ❻ *Volendammer Vishandel*.

Take a right at the pedestrian-only Eerste van der Helststraat, passing through Gerard Douplein, then head west to wholesale flower shop ❼ *Bloemenhandel Sijmons*. Here you can buy a bouquet of wild flowers away from the Albert Cuyp crowds. Double back and enjoy an afternoon of shopping at an array of independent retailers, including concept store ❽ *Felice Home of Brands*. Next, head north along the pretty Frans Halsstraat and browse the collection of English secondhand books at ❾ *Fenix Books*.

Stroll north for three blocks to Parisian-bistro-style ❿ *Café Caron*. Chef Alain Caron and his sons serve a range of rustic French classics, including escargots and charcuterie platters.

End the evening with a nightcap at the Netherlands' first winebar, ⓫ *Wijnbar Boelen & Boelen*. Reach it by walking east on Eerste Jacob van Campenstraat, then cutting across the Marie Heinekenplein (with the Heineken Brewery looming above) and turning right onto Eerste van der Helststraat.

Resources
—— Inside knowledge

This is a small city with plenty to offer visitors so to help you make the most of it we've compiled a few pertinent tips. Here's a round-up of how to navigate the canals, things to do come rain or shine and the calendar of events to plan your trip around. We've also put together a classic Amsterdam playlist and some useful words to get you under the skin of Dutch culture.

Transport
Get around town

01 Train: This is the fastest way to get into the city from Schiphol Airport, with frequent trains reaching Centraal station in about 20 minutes. *ns.nl*

02 Bicycle: Amsterdam is ideally set up for cyclists and there are plenty of rental shops to choose from. Familiarise yourself with road rules before heading out (*see page 14*).

03 Tram: Other than by bicycle, this is the most convenient way to travel. The conductor's booth at the back of each tram sells one-hour, 24-hour and 48-hour travel cards that are valid on trams, buses and the metro. Those with an I Amsterdam City Card (which also gives you museum entry) travel free. The 9292 website is a good place to start planning your journey. *9292.nl*

04 Bus: The slow but extensive bus network reaches far into Amsterdam's suburbs. Night buses no longer accept cash.

05 Metro: The five metro lines are great for getting out of the centre. Line 51 is the most useful, running from Centraal through the east, south and west. Line 52 is perfect for exploring the north.

06 Ferry: All GVB public-transport ferries crossing the IJ river north are free, with line 901/907 running all night. You can take your bicycle on board, of course. *ilovenoord.com/ferry*

07 Taxis and cars: Taxi ranks are plentiful and can be found throughout the city, while Uber and similar apps will show other taxi options. Parking is difficult and expensive, particularly in the centre, but if you must drive then it's more practical to use the park-and-ride schemes around the city. *iamsterdam.com*

Vocabulary
Local lingo

Most Dutch people speak fluent English but just in case, here are some key words. Quick tip: "j" is like "y" in "yacht".

01 Hallo/hoi: Hello/hi
02 Dank je wel: Thank you
03 Dag/doei: Bye
04 Proost: Cheers
05 Jammer: Too bad
06 Potverdorie: Damn
07 Nog een biertje/wijn: One more beer/wine
08 Mijn fiets is kapot: My bike is broken

Soundtrack to the city
Five top tunes

From a track by a homegrown house heavyweight to a moving French tribute to Dutch mariners, our soundtrack to Amsterdam is as varied as the city itself.

01 The Beatles, 'The Ballad of John and Yoko': They memorialised their infamous world peace "bed-in" at the Amsterdam Hilton so this is a reminder of the city's counter-cultural history.

02 Jacques Brel, 'Amsterdam': A song about the seedy underside of the city's mercantile backbone and the human cost of that success. David Bowie later recorded an English version.

03 MC Miker G & DJ Sven, 'Holiday Rap': A one-hit wonder from 1986 with two Dutch guys rapping over a Madonna sample. Pure and cheesy good times.

04 Tiesto, 'Adagio for Strings': Both industrially modern and historically poignant, this club banger from the Dutch electronic dance-music icon hits all the right notes.

05 The Ex, 'Squat!': This fired-up track from the Dutch punks captures the anger that fuelled a notable squatting scene in the 1980s.

Best events
What to see

01 Keukenhof: The world's largest flower gardens (located between the city and The Hague) open every spring so you can admire fields full of tulips.
March, keukenhof.nl

02 Restaurant Week: Look out for discounted menus across the city.
March and September, restaurantweek.nl

03 King's Day: A national celebration turns Amsterdam into a sea of orange with citywide street parties.
27 April

04 Taste of Amsterdam: Foodie festival in Amstelpark offering tasting dishes from some of the best chefs.
June, tasteofamsterdam.com

05 Holland Festival: Biggest and oldest international arts festival in the Netherlands, with theatre, dance, music, opera, film and much more.
June, hollandfestival.nl

06 Open Garden Days: A chance to peek at the private gardens and interiors of some canal houses.
June, opentuinendagen.nl

07 Kwaku Festival: A multicultural event commemorating the abolition of slavery in Dutch colonies, with music, food, markets, football and dance.
July-August, kwakufestival.nl

08 Gay Pride: One of the biggest and best pride celebrations in the world, with a week of exhibitions, parties and events that peaks with the Canal Parade.
July-August, pride.amsterdam

09 Amsterdam Heritage Days: Historical buildings, monuments and homes throw open their doors to the public free of charge.
September, amsterdam.nl

10 International Documentary Film Festival Amsterdam: The biggest festival of its kind in the world.
November, idfa.nl

Rainy days
Weather-proof activities

01 Culture galore: Amsterdam is brimming with excellent museums and galleries, from the Stedelijk to Rembrandthuis. The oft-overlooked Tropenmuseum (Museum of the Tropics), tucked away in a beautiful old building next to Oosterpark, is another wonderful option with several floors of fascinating objects, photographs, music, film and interactive displays about non-western culture. The regularly changing exhibits look at themes such as mourning, celebration and prayer. It's particularly good for children.
tropenmuseum.nl

02 Explore Westergasfabriek: The former gasworks complex in west Amsterdam has numerous things to do if the weather takes a turn for the worse. Browse a food market, join a yoga class, enjoy mussels and a gin and tonic, sit for some wine-tasting, catch an indie film, play arcade games while you nibble on Japanese food, visit the brewery or watch some live jazz. The architecture of the red-brick buildings is an interesting attraction in itself.
westergasfabriek.nl

03 Take to the water: Amsterdam still manages to look charming in the rain and if the weather is awful while you're visiting, a great way to sightsee and stay dry is to join a canal boat tour. Operator Rederij P Kooij is nearly a century old and remains a family business, offering informative hour-long tours of the city centre for a reasonable rate in fully covered boats. Its impressive guestbook includes famous names such as Winston Churchill, Michael Jackson and Nelson Mandela.
rederijkooij.nl

Sunny days
The great outdoors

01 Park life: Amsterdammers love their parks and Vondelpark in the south of the city, with its wending waterways and secluded spots, remains a beautiful place to while away an afternoon. Barbecues have recently been banned but picnics are still allowed and there are several good cafés to choose from if you haven't pre-packed your food and drink. Look out for Picasso's sculpture "The Fish", tucked away in a corner of the park.
hetvondelpark.net

02 Cycle it out: Offering a scenic respite from the bustle of Amsterdam, Ouderkerk aan de Amstel is about a half-hour cycle from the city centre yet it feels a world away. The quaint village dates back to the 12th century and is home to historical churches, the De Zwaan windmill and a 400-year-old Jewish cemetery, the oldest in the Netherlands. The trip takes you along the banks of the Amstel River, from which Amsterdam takes its name.

03 Beach day: Although the city has its fair share of great urban beaches such as Pllek (*see page 31*), nothing beats the real thing. When the weather warms up one of the most popular places to go is Bloemendaal aan Zee, a short train ride from the city. A range of wind and water sports are on offer here, including kitesurfing, stand-up paddle boarding and catamaran sailing. The beach has several upmarket bars and beach clubs offering everything from snacks to sophisticated lunches. When the sun goes down you can kick back with a cocktail, enjoy some relaxed dining or join in with one of the lively beach parties, outdoor cinema events or live gigs.

About Monocle
—— Step inside

London HQ
—
Our editorial office is in Marylebone

In 2007, Monocle was launched as a monthly magazine briefing on global affairs, business, culture, design and much more. We believed there was a globally minded audience of readers who were hungry for opportunities and experiences beyond their national borders.

Today Monocle is a complete media brand with print, audio and online elements – not to mention our expanding network of shops and cafés. Besides our London HQ we have international bureaux in Toronto, Tokyo, Zürich, Hong Kong and Los Angeles, with more on the way. We continue to grow and flourish and at our core is the simple belief that there will always be a place for a print brand that is committed to telling fresh stories and sending photographers on assignments. It's also a case of knowing that our success is all down to the readers, advertisers and collaborators who have supported us along the way.

❶
International bureaux
Boots on the ground

We're based in London and have bureaux in Hong Kong, Tokyo, Zürich, Toronto and Los Angeles, with more to come. We also call upon reports from our contributors in more than 35 cities around the world. For this guide, Mikaela Aitken, Nolan Giles, Joleen Goffin and Venetia Rainey decamped to the Dutch capital to explore all that it has to offer. They also called on the many contacts in their address book to ensure that we've covered the best in food, culture and more.

❷
Online
Digital delivery

We have a dynamic website: *monocle.com*. As well as being the place to hear our radio station, Monocle 24, the site presents our films, which are beautifully shot and edited by our in-house team and provide a fresh perspective on our stories. Check out the films celebrating the cities that make up our Travel Guide Series before you explore the rest of the site.

❸
Retail and cafés
Food for thought

Via our shops in Toronto, Zürich, Tokyo, London, Los Angeles and Hong Kong – including one in the airport (*pictured*) – we sell products that cater to our readers' tastes and are produced in collaboration with brands we believe in. We also have cafés in Tokyo, Zürich and London. And if you are in the UK capital visit the Kioskafé in Paddington, which combines good coffee and great reads.

Print
Committed to the page

MONOCLE is published 10 times a year. We also produce two standalone publications – THE FORECAST, packed with insights into the year ahead, and THE ESCAPIST – plus seasonal weekly newspapers and an annual *Drinking & Dining Directory*. Since 2013 we have also been publishing travel guides, like this one, and bigger books. Visit *monocle.com/shop*.

Radio
Sound approach

Monocle 24 is our round-the-clock radio station that was launched in 2011. It delivers global news and shows covering foreign affairs, urbanism, business, culture, food and drink, design and print media. Our eclectic playlists will also accompany you day and night. You can listen live or download any of our shows from *monocle.com*, iTunes or SoundCloud.

Join the club

01
Subscribe to Monocle
A subscription is a simple way to make sure that you never miss an issue – and you'll enjoy many additional benefits.

02
Be in the know
Our subscribers have exclusive access to the entire Monocle archive, and priority access to selected product collaborations, at *monocle.com*.

03
Stay in the loop
Subscription copies are delivered to your door at no extra cost no matter where you are in the world. We also offer an auto-renewal service to ensure that you never miss an issue.

04
And there's more...
Subscribers benefit from a 10 per cent discount at all Monocle shops, including online, and receive exclusive offers and invitations to events around the world.

Choose your package

Premium one year
13 × issues
+ Porter Sub Club bag

One year
12 × issues
+ Monocle Voyage tote bag

Six months
6 × issues

Chief photographer
Jussi Puikkonen

Still life
David Sykes

Writers
Mikaela Aitken
Carole Baijings
Sanne Bolten
Robert Bound
Melkon Charchoglyan
Yoko Choy
Sabine de Witte
Hans den Hartog Jager
Pauline den Hartog Jager
Ramiro Espinoza
Nolan Giles
Joleen Goffin
Vicky Hampton
Daphne Karnezis
Pete Kempshall
Marie-Anne Leuty
Brian Maston
Mirik Milan
Alice Pfeiffer
Dan Poole
Venetia Rainey
Chiara Rimella
Marie-Sophie Schwarzer
Hester Underhill

Images
Roos Aldershoff
Annelore Photography
Benthem Crouwel Architects
Arjan Bronkhorst
Christiaan de Bruijne
Ellen de Bruijne Projects
Fred Ernst
Luuk Kramer
John Lewis Marshall
Jannes Linders
Matteo Rossi
Ruud Splinter
Rob 't Hart
Marcel van der Burg
Ton van Namen
Gert Jan van Rooi
David De Vleeschauwer

Illustrators
Satoshi Hashimoto
Ceylan Sahin Eker
Tokuma

Monocle
EDITOR IN CHIEF AND CHAIRMAN
Tyler Brûlé
EDITOR
Andrew Tuck
CREATIVE DIRECTOR
Richard Spencer Powell

**The Monocle Travel Guide
Series: Amsterdam**
GUIDE EDITOR
Mikaela Aitken
ASSOCIATE GUIDE EDITORS
Nolan Giles
Joleen Goffin
PHOTO EDITOR
Victoria Cagol

**The Monocle Travel Guide
Series**
SERIES EDITOR
Joe Pickard
ASSOCIATE EDITOR
Chloë Ashby
ASSISTANT EDITOR
Hester Underhill
DESIGNER
Giulia Tugnoli
PHOTO EDITOR
Victoria Cagol

CHAPTER EDITING

Need to know
Mikaela Aitken
Pauline den Hartog Jager

Hotels
Mikaela Aitken

Food and drink
Venetia Rainey

Retail
Nolan Giles

Things we'd buy
Mikaela Aitken
Nolan Giles

Essays
Mikaela Aitken
Pauline den Hartog Jager

Culture
Mikaela Aitken

Design and architecture
Mikaela Aitken

Sport and fitness
Mikaela Aitken

Walks
Mikaela Aitken

Resources
Venetia Rainey

Research
Melkon Charchoglyan
Tom Furse
Naomi Joseph
Ian Keddie
Charles McFarlane
Aliz Tennant
Ceinwen Thomas

Special thanks
Arcam
Kathy Ball
Yoko Choy
Sabine de Witte
Yana Foqué
Aron Friedman
High Studios
I Amsterdam
Pete Kempshall
Rhiannon Pickles
Amy Richardson
Sanne Visser
Shanthi Voorn
X Bank